Taste of Latvia

Hippocrene is NUMBER ONE in
International Cookbooks

Africa and Oceania
Best of Regional African Cooking
Egyptian Cooking
Good Food from Australia
Traditional South African Cookery
Taste of Eritrea

Asia and Near East
Afghan Food and Cookery
Best of Goan Cooking
Best of Kashmiri Cooking
The Joy of Chinese Cooking
The Art of South Indian Cooking
The Indian Spice Kitchen
The Art of Persian Cooking
The Art of Israeli Cooking
The Art of Turkish Cooking
The Art of Uzbek Cooking

Mediterranean
Best of Greek Cuisine
Taste of Malta
A Spanish Family Cookbook
Tastes of North Africa

Western Europe
Art of Dutch Cooking
Best of Austrian Cuisine
A Belgian Cookbook
Cooking in the French Fashion
  (bilingual)
Celtic Cookbook
English Royal Cookbook
The Swiss Cookbook
Traditional Recipes from Old
  England
The Art of Irish Cooking
Traditional Food from Scotland
Traditional Food from Wales
The Scottish-Irish Pub and Hearth
  Cookbook
A Treasury of Italian Cuisine
  (bilingual)

Scandinavia
Best of Scandinavian Cooking
The Best of Finnish Cooking
The Best of Smorgasbord Cooking
Good Food from Sweden

Central Europe
Best of Albanian Cooking
Best of Croatian Cooking
All Along the Danube
Bavarian Cooking
Traditional Bulgarian Cooking
The Best of Czech Cooking
The Best of Slovak Cooking
The Art of Hungarian Cooking
Art of Lithuanian Cooking
Polish Heritage Cookery
The Best of Polish Cooking
Old Warsaw Cookbook
Old Polish Traditions
Treasury of Polish Cuisine
  (bilingual)
Poland's Gourmet Cuisine
Taste of Romania
Taste of Latvia

Eastern Europe
The Cuisine of Armenia
The Best of Russian Cooking
Traditional Russian Cuisine
  (bilingual)
The Best of Ukrainian Cuisine

Americas
Cooking the Caribbean Way
Mayan Cooking
The Honey Cookbook
The Art of Brazilian Cookery
The Art of South American
  Cookery
Old Havana Cookbook
  (bilingual)

Taste of Latvia

BY
Siri Lise Doub

PHOTOGRAPHS BY
Gill Holland

COVER PHOTOGRAPH BY
Astri Kollme

HIPPOCRENE BOOKS, INC.
New York

ISBN 0-7818-0803-0

For information, contact:
HIPPOCRENE BOOKS, INC.
171 Madison Avenue
New York, NY 10016

Printed in the United States of America.

For Robb
Who shows me the world

ACKNOWLEDGEMENTS

Much thanks to my extraordinary family, but most especially to my husband, Robb, for his support and to my wonderful father who patiently read and re-read the manuscript and provided invaluable assistance and beautiful photographs every step of the way.

A special thanks to Robin Hanna, without whom this book would not have been possible.

Grateful acknowledgement is also made to Carol Chitnis, Managing Editor at Hippocrene Books, Ieva Liepniece, Joanna Ciszewska, Amanda MacDonnell, Anita Plesuma, Andzelika Gudone, Uldis Jaunzems-Petersons, and Zoja Klujeva.

CONTENTS

vii

My child, we are a nation of eaters, but put your spoon down in your bowl while a song is being sung. Don't look at that man eating, don't learn from him. He has eaten all his songs. He can't tell the difference between songs and lettuce.

—Imants Ziedonis, Latvian poet

INTRODUCTION

Very little is known of Latvia. Although an ancient ethnic cultural area, as a nation it is young in years. Many of us are vague about its location ... language ... culture ... history. The purpose of this book is to introduce the personality of Latvia through cuisine and culture, and thus help preserve its wonders.

I quickly discovered while in Latvia that its national cuisine is not as bland as most people (including Latvians) proclaim it to be. Although it is a simple but hearty fare, the often-used homegrown seasonings like cream, dill, caraway, nuts, and onions do add plenty of flavor (although Latvians themselves have been known to "spice up a dish by adding mayonnaise"). You'll find most prevalent in Latvian cooking are dairy foods, porridges, pork, potatoes, and, of course, the famous Latvian rye bread and cottage cheese, staples in the diet of any good Latvian farmer.

Cuisine is only one part of a nation's personality. On paper Latvia, a relatively new nation, celebrates its ninth birthday this year. Its centuries-old history and traditions, however, are vividly alive in modern Latvia. Consider the country's history. Its situation at the crossroads of western and eastern Europe has given it an advantageous but somewhat precarious position. The battleground for countless struggles throughout the centuries, Latvia has been invaded by the Germans, Poles, Swedes, Russians, and Napoleonic French. Maps have called it Terra Mariana, Livonia, Livland, Courland, and Lettgallia before today's Latvia. Yet amazingly the spirit of the Latvian people has kept their distinctive national identity alive in spite of centuries of foreign dominance.

Second, consider its culture. As you'll notice, I've sprinkled folk songs, or *dainas*, throughout the book. They were plucked

1

from a collection of about a million and half gathered over the last century or so. These folk songs, which are an integal part of Latvian life, represent Latvians in every sense: at home, in the field, at festivals and festivities. Early Latvian literature was entirely oral. The first Latvian dictionary didn't appear until the 17th century, and the first Latvian-language newspapers in the beginning of the 19th century. Therefore the *dainas*, songs of daily life, spiritual awakenings, hopes, fears, and yearly events, provide invaluable insight into Latvian history and culture. I fell in love with them. With the help of the librarians at the National Library and Lettonica, a room dedicated to Latvian studies, I discovered an ample supply of English-language translations. In fact, *Latvian Folk Songs*, which I found to be particularly helpful, was written in part and edited by Vaira Vikis-Freibergs, the recently elected President of Latvia who is the first woman President in the former Soviet Union. A former professor of psychology in Montreal, she fled Latvia at the end of World War II to a German refugee camp and eventually to Canada. Along with many Latvian émigrés, she returned after independence and before being elected president was director of the Latvian Institute, a non-government organization that promotes the image of the country overseas. In the book she proclaims that the "live" daina, or one sung in context or performed, is far superior than the written one, "a faded flower pressed between the pages of grandmother's hymnal." Although I agree, I was so drawn to their beauty and warmth that I couldn't resist including written versions in these pages.

I have also included ancient Latvian symbols, another clue to Latvia's culture, at the beginning of each chapter. In ancient Latvia the Baltic and Finno-Ugric tribes gave names and symbols, or *zime*, to their deities, who played a constant role in daily life. These symbols formed the foundation of Latvian folk art. Today they still adorn folk costumes, leather goods, buildings, and other objects and clothing. Latvians throughout the world know the meaning and superstitions attached to the symbols. "I never greet anyone over the threshold—even in Australia," one Latvian-Australian told me. "It's bad luck to disturb Laima. And Jāņi (Midsummer Nights' festival, see page 226), which celebrates the sun, is practiced on June 23—the middle of winter—in Australia as well—even though we are often freezing and our neighbors think we're crazy!"

Ancient *dainas* and symbols tell us a great deal about Latvian culture. But Latvia's many occupiers also influenced her culture, language, and especially cuisine. *Pīrāgi*, for example, although common throughout Latvia, probably came from the Russian dumpling called *pirozhki*. Not surprising when you consider the enormous number of Russians still living in Latvia because of mass deportation of Latvians to Siberia and the large influx of Russian workers during Soviet times. (Before Soviet occupation, Latvians made up about 75% of the population. By 1989 the figure was 51%.) The number of Russians—and their contribution to local cuisine—surprise returning Latvians émigrés. I talked to one Latvian who fled Riga in the back of a goat-driven car to a refugee camp in Germany in the 1940s. Upon her recent return to retire in Latvia, she expressed her shock at hearing so much Russian spoken in the streets. "Some people *only* speak Russian," she said in disbelief.

When studying Latvia, it's easy to dwell on Latvia's most recent history. I was certain that a portion of the book would have to include stories of the tragedy of Latvia's lost independence in 1939 and the horrors of life under the Soviet system. My Latvian friends, however, persuaded me that their testimonies of oppression—whether under the Soviets or under other foreign rule—do not in any way reflect the culture and the people of Latvia. I acquiesced, and have done my best to concentrate on pure Latvian ancient culture.

A final note about modern Latvia. It is a complex and often misunderstood nation. This period of independence has not yet become the rosy, prosperous picture of Latvia's first independence in the 1920s when Latvia was the second in Europe in grain production per capita, third in number of livestock, and held top places in Europe in respect to the number of students and published books. Many Latvians begrudgingly told me that the new independence could prove difficult. One friend explained, "We breathed in one breath during the independence movement ... but we cannot always ride the wave." Many believe that it will take a generation for the country to see the kind of prosperity it remembers from the 1920s. For most, however, it is worth it. A venture capitalist in Riga told me that he remembers taking his first trip west while under the Soviet eye. He compared it to taking off a blindfold. "There was more in the gas stations in Finland than in our stores," he remarked. Another friend said that after shopping during a school trip to Germany, she returned to her hotel and wept. I feel sure that the strength and perseverance of the Latvian people, which have been proven by recent history as well as its centuries of culture and pride, will enable the country eventually to claim victory. The Latvians have worked hard for freedom.

I hope this book serves to introduce not only Latvian cuisine but also the vibrant history of the country to readers.

Labu apetiti!

A NOTE ABOUT DAINAS

Latvian folk songs, or *dainas,* probably the strongest cultural component in Latvia, tell us much about ancient Latvians and their beliefs. They enable us to understand modern Latvians as well. More than one and a half million oral songs, first collected and recorded in the late 19th century by the scholar Krišjānis Barons (affectionately known as Father Barons, or *Barontēvs),* reflect the ancient spirit of *dzives zina.* This attitude toward one's self, others, and the world was the root of ancient Latvian culture. *Dainas* also reflect the belief still held by many today that the whole world is *dievota,* or saturated in divine spirit.

Dainas, which represent various stages of the cycle of life and nature, sing of the gods that participate in each stage of life and the strong tie the Latvians hold with land, animals, and the seasons. In ancient times one god, Dievs, "Bright Sky," figured prominently. Mara (Mother), Laime (Fate), Perkons (Thunder), Saule (Sun), and Jumis (the symbol for eternal or recurring life) were also important deities addressed in *dainas.*

As my friend Zoja, a member of the Skandinieki folklore ensemble, the 1993 winners of Europe's award for contributions to national culture, pointed out, the constant domination of Latvia throughout history by one warring tribe or another only served to strengthen the Latvian inner culture. During centuries of oppression, *dainas,* which sang of folk tales, culture, and spirit, were a source of consolidation for Latvians. The tragic loss of independence 50 years ago, which had been achieved in 1919 for barely 20 years, also served to renew a sense of national pride and determination to keep the Latvian culture alive. The ancient religion Dievturiba, for example, whose members believe that theirs is the only truly Latvian religion, Christianity

5

being the religion of invaders, thrived during the Soviet era. In those days it was a crime to practice any religion; most churches were used for museums and conference centers. Such "nationalism" did not come without a price, however. Dievturiba was monitored closely by the KGB. One leader spent 22 years in Soviet prisons. Although not a member of Dievturiba, Zoja herself was asked to leave the school where she was teaching when the KGB discovered that she was teaching traditional *dainas* to her students. Today her folklore ensemble performs all over the world and teaches monthly culture classes at the Sena Klets traditional costume store in Riga. Dievturiba also holds periodic gatherings at Riga's National History Museum.

Salads

Dievs
God or Heaven

The presence of God or heaven as love and goodness is widely proclaimed in *dainas*. Dievs or "Bright Sun" promotes fertility especially of grain crops and fields. The base of the symbol for Dievs represents the earth, and its circle God reigning above the heavens. The symbol has been found on metal jewelry dating from the Early Iron Age.

As council and participant in human activities, Dievs figures prominently:

Augstāk dzied cīrulīts	Higher sings the lark
Aiz visiem putniņiem;	Than any other bird.
Dievam gudris padomiņš	Dievs holds wise council
Par šo visu pasaulīt'.	Over the whole of this world.

—Latvian folk song

In the spring and summer months Latvians in the countryside live off the mouth-wateringly tender vegetables that practically fall from the garden vine. One bright May day, I visited my friend Ieva's farm outside Rauna. There we feasted on rhubarb, cucumbers, and tomatoes picked straight from her garden, milk still warm from the cow, honey from the bees, and sour cream made from the fresh milk—and I've never tasted anything better. In Rīga the best place to buy vegetables is at the bustling Central Market located in a series of former Zeppelin hangers beside the railway station. Farmers from miles around come to sell their produce here. You can find everything from pig's heads and live lobsters to leather pants, lizards, and lilies.

After we packed away the leftovers of a large lunch in the underground cellar that serves as the refrigerator, we took a walk around the countryside, stopping first to watch Ieva's aunt and uncle feed the bees and gather the honey in the apiary. A kilometer or so farther we happened upon the ruins of a 13th-century castle, once the summer residence of Bishop Albert, who founded Rīga in 1201. The castle ruins are connected to the hills near Ieva's house by a series of long tunnels, used in Albert's time for mistresses, quick escapes, and other shifty business.

On the way home from a brief spelunk, Ieva pointed out an old roadside memorial to the Soviet soldiers who had died defending Rauna from the Germans. During Soviet times Ieva and her classmates were expected to keep the monument area weeded, swept, and polished. Today the area is overgrown and the monument dull.

Selling honey in Rīga's Central Market.

Tomato Salad

3 cups chopped tomato (about 4 medium tomatoes)
1 cup sour cream
fresh parsley
chives
salt
pepper

1. Mix chopped tomatoes with sour cream.
2. Add parsley, chives, salt, and pepper to taste.

Refrigerate before serving.

MAKES 3 TO 4 SERVINGS.

I love a leafy garden
Green with the light of May.
—Latvian poet Plūdonis

Cucumber Salad

2½ cups chopped cucumber (about 2 large cucumbers)
1 cup sour cream
fresh parsley
chives
salt
pepper

1. Mix chopped cucumbers with sour cream.
2. Add parsley, chives, salt, and pepper to taste.

Refrigerate before serving.

MAKES 3 TO 4 SERVINGS.

Ieva's Countryside Potato Salad

about 15 boiled potatoes, peeled and diced
1½ cups chopped pickles (10 to 12 small pickles)
1¼ cups chopped cucumber (about 1 large cucumber)
2 cups corn
2 cups peas
½ cup sour cream
salt
pepper
¾ cup chopped onion (1 medium onion; optional)
3 tablespoons hot mustard (optional)
3 teaspoons mayonnaise (optional)
2 eggs, hard-boiled and halved

1. Mix potatoes, pickles, cucumber, corn, and peas with sour cream.
2. Add salt and pepper to taste. For more flavor, add the onion mixed with the mustard and mayonnaise.

Garnish with the hard-boiled egg sections.

MAKES 8 TO 10 SERVINGS.

ANCIENT LATVIAN SPRINGTIME BELIEF: If you hear a cuckoo on an empty stomach on the first day of spring, you'll be hungry all year. If you hear the cuckoo with no money in your pocket, you'll be penniless the year-round.

When you order a salad in Latvia or most East European countries, don't expect the iceberg lettuce and Italian dressing variations you'll find in the West. Rather, the Latvians use sour cream and lots of it to flavor their salads. They often don't use lettuce at all. The following leafy green salad, however, is traditional Latvian. Although it is served with the usual sour cream and kefir dressing, it is the closest you'll find to a Western salad. The other simple vegetable salads listed here are purely Latvian fare.

Osiris café, my favorite in Rīga, is the third of a slew of restaurants owned by Andrejs Žagars, director of the National Opera. Located in an unassuming building outside Old Rīga on the corner of K. Barona and Lāčplēša ielas, this quietly elegant—and inexpensive—café is a regular hangout of artists and writers and serves up delicious Latvian fare and seafood dishes as well as many good salads. It also has one of the best breakfast menus in the Baltic. The former theater and film actor Žagars was instrumental in reviving Latvia's opera after the 1991 independence.

Lettuce Salad

1 head Boston lettuce, cut in small pieces
¼ cup sour cream
1 cup kefir (substitute: Greek yogurt)
fresh parsley, chopped fine
fresh chives, chopped fine
fresh dill, chopped fine
salt
pepper
1 egg, hard-boiled (optional)
juice from 1 lemon (optional)

1. Mix chopped lettuce with sour cream, kefir, parsley, chives, and dill. Refrigerate about 15 minutes so that the tastes blend.
2. Add salt and pepper to taste. Refrigerate before serving.

Garnish with sliced hard-boiled egg and lemon juice if desired.

MAKES 4 SERVINGS.

Beet Salad

½ cup sour cream
1 tablespoon mayonnaise
¼ cup finely chopped onions
salt
pepper
1 cup peeled and cooked beets
1 cup peeled and chopped apples
1 cup chopped celery
fresh parsley

1. Mix the sour cream, mayonnaise, and onions. Add salt and pepper to taste.
2. Mix beets, apples, and celery. Mix lightly with sour cream dressing. Garnish with parsley.

MAKES 5 TO 6 SERVINGS.

Coleslaw with Apples

1 teaspoon salt
4 cups grated cabbage
juice from 1 lemon
2 red apples, diced
1 large carrot, chopped
2 tablespoons chopped fresh parsley
½ cup sour cream
1 or 2 tablespoons mayonnaise
1 teaspoon sugar

1. Sprinkle salt over cabbage in a bowl. Pour boiling water over cabbage until covered. Let stand for 15 minutes. Drain and pat dry.
2. Pour lemon juice over chopped apples. Mix with cabbage, chopped carrots, and parsley.
3. In a small bowl, mix sour cream, mayonnaise, and sugar. Add to cabbage mixture and mix well. Refrigerate for several hours before serving.

MAKES 5 TO 6 SERVINGS.

Sauerkraut Salad
with Apples and Carrots

1 cup sauerkraut
1 cup grated carrots
½ cup grated apples
1 onion, grated
½ sour cream
salt
sugar

1. Mix sauerkraut, carrots, apples, and onion together.
2. Mix sour cream with salt and sugar to taste. Mix with salad.

MAKES 4 TO 5 SERVINGS.

Stuffed Tomatoes

You may substitute any of these vegetables with others you prefer. Cooked carrots and corn are also good.

2 cups cooked peas
2 apples, peeled and diced
1 cup chopped sweet pickles (about 8 pickles)
8 ounces cooked milk sausage, cut in small pieces
    (substitute: baloney or ham)
4 eggs, hard-boiled and cut in small pieces
5 boiled potatoes, peeled and diced
¾ cup sour cream
¾ cup mayonnaise
salt
7 medium, firm tomatoes

1. For salad stuffing, mix peas, apples, pickles, sausage, eggs, and potatoes together.
2. Add sour cream and mayonnaise. Mix well. Add salt to taste.
3. Cut off the tops of each tomato and, using a serrated spoon, remove the pulp and seeds. The tomato walls should be strong enough to support the stuffing. Stuff the tomatoes with the salad mixture. Cover each tomato with top.

MAKES 7 SERVINGS.

Mushroom Stuffing Variation:

Autumn is the best time for gathering mushrooms in Latvia, and you'll often see mushroom pickers in the forests from August through October.

1 or 2 cups wild mushrooms, chopped or 2 cans
    (8 ounces each) mushrooms, chopped
1 teaspoon tarragon leaves
2 tablespoons white vinegar
1 teaspoon sugar
salt
pepper
1 cup sour cream
chives, dill, or parsley

1. Mix mushrooms, tarragon, vinegar, and sugar together.
2. Add salt and pepper to taste. Refrigerate at least 2 hours.
3. Before serving, add sour cream to mixture. Fill tomatoes. Garnish with chives, dill, or parsley.

Stewed Cabbage

1 head white cabbage
oil or lard for frying
salt

1. Wash the cabbage and remove the leaves. Cut into small pieces.
2. In a frying pan, stew cabbage with oil over medium heat until the leaves are brown on all sides. Add a small amount of water if necessary. Add salt to taste.

MAKES 3 TO 4 SERVINGS.

ANCIENT LATVIAN BELIEF: The spirits of the deceased will trail you home from the cemetery. People believed that these spirits could cause harm, and visitors covered their tracks so they would not be followed. Today many Latvian cemeteries are still skirted by sandy paths that are raked smooth after each visit to keep the graveyard neat ... and to remove footprints.

The Turaida Dainu Kalns, or Folk Song Hill, is home to 24 sculptures designed by Latvian sculptor Indulis Ranka in 1985 for the 150th anniversary of Krišjānis Barons' birth. Many believe that the Song Father (see p. 49) is a metaphor for the nation's silent yearning for freedom; when Ranka created the sculpture, there were still no signs of the approaching revolution of 1991. Others perceive the Song Father as the ancient Latvian god who, according to folk tales, wanders the rye fields in a gray coat. On the other side of the Song Father sculpture is Spidola, whose Latvian folk character symbolizes the spirit of the nation.

One September Sunday we spent a delightful afternoon at Mr. Ranka's house, where he showed us the tools with which he "releases" the many sculptures that surround his home. Although he studied as a painter, he discovered artistic "freedom from professors and classrooms" in sculpture early and has become Latvia's most renowned sculptor. He truly enjoys art for art's sake and receives no money for his work at Turaida and many other locales.

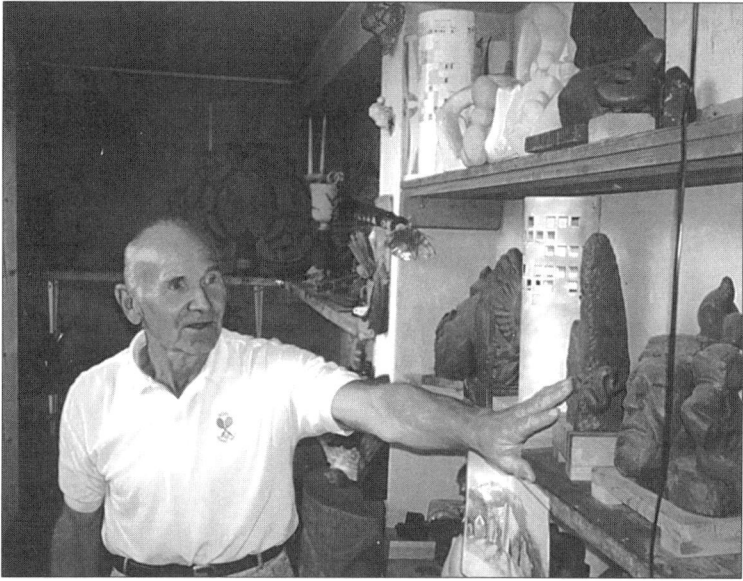

Indulis Ranka in his studio.

Sculptures in Dainu Kalns.

Beet and Apple Salad

Biesu un abolu salati

Serve with boiled potatoes or sliced potatoes fried in milk butter (or regular butter if milk butter is not available). Many Latvians boil the potatoes before frying them. Variations to the dish are also popular. Some Latvians add lemon, cooked carrots, garlic, or minced walnuts before serving.

3 small red beets
1½ teaspoons salt
2 apples, peeled
1½ cups sour cream
salt
pepper
1 teaspoon sugar
mayonnaise (optional)

1. Boil unpeeled beets in about 12 cups water with the salt for about 30 minutes or bake in oven at 350 degrees F in baking pan sealed with foil 45 minutes to 1 hour or until soft. Place under cold water for 10 minutes.
2. Peel and grate cooked beets coarsely.
3. Grate apples coarsely. Mix beets and apples.
4. Add sour cream. Mix well. Add salt and pepper to taste.
5. Sprinkle sugar over salad before serving. If the salad tastes sour, add mayonnaise.

MAKES 4 TO 6 SERVINGS.

Cabbage Salad or Latvian Coleslaw

1 small bottle (4 ounces) horseradish
¾ cup sour cream
2 apples, peeled
4 cups grated savoy cabbage (about ½ head)
¾ to 1 cup grated carrot (4 to 5 medium carrots)
pepper
salt
gar

1. Mix horseradish and sour cream in large bowl.
2. Grate apples coarsely and add to horseradish and sour cream.
3. In a separate bowl, mix cabbage and carrots with pepper to taste.
4. Mix all ingredients well. Add salt and more pepper to taste, if necessary.
5. Sprinkle sugar over salad before serving.

MAKES 4 TO 6 SERVINGS.

Es piesēju kumeliņu
Pie ziedošas ābelītes,
Nobierst manis kumeliņis
Ar ābeles ziediņiem.
Jāju, jāju pa celiņu
Ar ziedošu kumeliņu.

I tied up my steed
To a blossoming apple tree,
My steed became dappled
With apple blossoms.
I went riding my way .
With a horse all abloom.

—Latvian folk song

Sculpture in Bastion Hill Park.

Cannellini Salad

2 cups chopped carrots (about 4 medium carrots)
2 apples, peeled and diced
2 medium cucumbers, peeled and chopped
1 can (15 ounces) cannellini beans
    (substitute: other white bean)
1 small bottle (4 ounces) horseradish
8 ounces sour cream
salt
pepper

1. Mix carrots, apples, cucumbers, and beans together.
2. In small bowl, mix horseradish and sour cream for dressing. Add to vegetable-apple mixture.
3. Add salt and pepper to taste.

VARIATION: You can also make a dressing by mixing 2 tablespoons mayonnaise and 3 tablespoons sour cream. Add pepper and salt to taste.

MAKES 4 TO 6 SERVINGS.

ANCIENT LATVIAN BELIEF: On Gerdacis Day (March 17) you must rise before the bears wake from hibernation or they will give you their sleepiness and you'll be sleepy all year-round.

I named this salad after Lolita, a lovely gray-haired country woman who moved from Rīga to Rauna 20 odd years ago to raise her small daughter. In the 1920s Lolita's parents built the house in which she lives today. With an elaborate hot-water system sourced by a wood-burning stove in the kitchen, its design was then one of the foremost of its time. The heat travels to each of the rooms, which also has a "hot seat" where you can sit and warm yourself during the long cold winters. Today the house is still heated this way.

When the Soviet troops arrived in 1939, Lolita's parents fled the house to join the resistance groups hiding in the forest. (By the end of World War II, 10,000 to 15,000 Latvians had sought refuge in the forests.) After a few months they returned to their home, which had since become part of a Soviet collective farm or *kolkhozes* with shared equipment, fields, and an allotted number of animals, as the system decreed.

Today the farm property is again Lolita's. Each morning and evening she attends to the apiary, three cows, the pigs, chickens, cats, and dogs. Although she lives off her land, she earns several lats a month by selling fresh milk to the local milk distributor. She leaves containers of fresh milk on a wooden stand at the end of her long driveway for weekly pick-ups. The distributors test the milk for quality, and she is paid accordingly.

꧁ꕥ꧂

Lolita's Potato Salad

about 15 boiled potatoes, peeled and diced
2 cups chopped cooked carrots (4 to 5 medium carrots)
2 cups corn
2 cups peas
2 eggs, hard-boiled and cut in small pieces
½ cup mayonnaise
1 cup sour cream
1 cup crabmeat
1 cup chopped sweet pickles (about 10 small pickles)
salt
pepper

1. Mix potatoes, carrots, corn, peas, eggs, mayonnaise, sour cream, crabmeat, and pickles.
2. Add salt and pepper to taste.

Refrigerate before serving.

MAKES 8 TO 10 SERVINGS.

John's Pickles

Jana marinetie gurki

5 to 10 cucumbers (or as many as will fit snugly in a jar)
¼ cup chopped black currant leaves
¼ cup crushed garlic
⅓ cup chopped fresh dill
2 tablespoons salt
1 tablespoon sugar
2 to 3 tablespoons strong vinegar (71% proof)

1. Fit cucumbers snugly in a jar. Layer black currant leaves, garlic, and dill, alternating until the jar is full.
2. Boil 4 cups water, salt, and sugar together. Pour into the jar over the pickles. Let cool.
3. Strain the water from the jar into a pot and bring the water to a boil again.
4. Before pouring the water back in the jar, add vinegar. If you plan to store the pickles for an entire season, add another tablespoon or so of vinegar to the water. Bring to a boil again.

Store the jars in a warm place. The pickles will be ready in 2 to 3 days. You can store them for up to a few years.

MAKES ONE 24-OUNCE JAR.

Breaded Cauliflower

·····································

½ head medium cauliflower, cleaned and
    cut in small pieces
½ cup (1 stick) butter
1 cup toasted bread crumbs (grated whole-grain,
    sugar-free Swedish toast is best)
salt

1. Fry cauliflower in butter over medium to high heat until cooked
   or fairly soft.
2. Remove from heat. Mix with crumbs. Add salt to taste.

MAKES 4 SERVINGS.

ANCIENT LATVIAN BELIEF: To keep your house free of flies,
clean it before sunrise on Binduksis Day (March 21).

Pea Salad

1 can (8.5 ounces) peas
4 tablespoons mayonnaise

Mix together for a simple and very popular side salad.

MAKES 4 SERVINGS.

Rīga's city canal.

Sweet Carrots
Karamesu burkani

1 cup (2 sticks) butter
3 tablespoons sugar
5 medium carrots, sliced lengthwise and boiled

1. Melt butter over medium heat. Add sugar, stirring constantly.
2. Fry carrots in butter for 3 to 5 minutes. Continue to stir constantly.

Serve slightly warm.

MAKES 4 SERVINGS.

ANCIENT LATVIAN CUSTOM: Many trees are still considered sacred in Latvia. The oak, for example, symbolizes masculinity. The linden symbolizes feminine virtues. When a baby is born, oak or linden branches are burned in order to give the baby the strengths he or she needs in life. In addition, oak leaves line the approach to the church at weddings.

Radish Salad

2 cups chopped radishes (about 15 radishes)
1½ cups chopped tomatoes (about 2 medium tomatoes)
⅓ large cucumber, peeled
2 cups sour cream
2 tablespoons dill
2 tablespoons chopped green onions

1. Mix chopped radish and tomatoes.
2. Slice cucumber down the middle. Scoop out seeds and pulp. Cut into small pieces.
3. Mix cucumbers, radishes, tomatoes, and sour cream.
4. Add dill and onion. Mix well.

MAKES 4 SERVINGS.

*B*reads
and
*P*īrāgi

Mara

The goddess Mara, who lives in the willow trees, has the powerful role of giving and taking life. Ancient Latvians warded off evil by offering black hens to Mara in the forests, rivers, springs, and sacred rocks she is said to embody. If a black hen wasn't available, rye bread and barley beer would suffice. Mara is also the patroness of cows and sheep.

Mara's cross, the symbol of the hearth

Mara's Fire Cross or Thunder Cross, which was recorded long before the Christian cross, offers protection from evil and symbolizes fire, thunder, fortune, health, and prosperity. It is often etched onto bread before baking to ensure a good loaf.

Māte, Māte, mīļa māte	Mother, dear mother
Ne tā mana mūža māte.	She is not my eternal mother.
Zemīt' mana mūža māte,	The earth is my mother,
Glabā manu augumiņu.	She looks after my body.

—Latvian folk song

Herb Bread
Zaḷumu maize

YEAST DOUGH
1 (¼-ounce) package dry yeast
4 cups wheat flour
1 cup whole milk
1 tablespoon butter or margarine
salt

FOR FILLING:
5 hard-boiled eggs
2 tablespoons chopped fresh parsley
2 tablespoons chopped fresh dill
2 tablespoons chopped fresh chervil
2 tablespoons chopped leeks
celery salt
pepper
2 teaspoons dried thyme
2 egg whites

1. To make yeast dough, first dissolve the yeast in warm water by letting it stand for 5 minutes. Add to flour. Heat milk, 1 cup water, and butter and let simmer. Add warm mixture to flour. Add salt and mix well. Cover with oiled plastic wrap or a damp, clean dish towel and set aside in draft-free, warm place (about 80 degrees F) to rise until doubled in size, 1 to 2 hours. (Or place pan of covered dough on rack over a large pan of hot, steaming water.)

2. Roll yeast dough flat, about ½ inch thick. Peel and chop eggs. Wash and chop parsley, dill, chervil, and leek. Mix with eggs. Add celery salt, pepper, and thyme.

3. Spread egg whites on dough. Sprinkle filling evenly over dough. Roll dough into a long French loaf. Set aside to rise, placing the end of roll face down. Let rise again at room temperature, until doubled, about 45 minutes.

4. Preheat oven to 375 degrees F. Bake for 30 to 40 minutes or until slightly brown.

MAKES 8 TO 10 SERVINGS.

ANCIENT LATVIAN BELIEF: You'll marry a farmer if you eat the heel of a loaf of bread.

Easy Rye Bread

For additional sour taste, use 1 cup starter dough (retained from a previous baking or made from 1 cup rye flour, 2 cups warm water, 1 (¼-ounce) package dry yeast, and ¼ cup yogurt).

2 cups whole milk
about 5 cups rye flour (to double the recipe,
　　use 2 cups white flour in addition to the rye)
1 (¼-ounce) package dry yeast
pinch of salt
2 tablespoons Crisco or other vegetable shortening
1 egg, beaten

1. Heat milk in a saucepan over medium heat. Add 2½ cups flour. Dissolve yeast in a little warm water by letting it stand for 5 minutes and add to saucepan. Mix well and cover with oiled plastic wrap or a damp, clean dish cloth and set aside in a draft-free, warm place (about 80 degrees F) to rise until doubled in size, 1 to 2 hours. (Or place pan of covered dough on rack over a large pan of hot, steaming water.) If desired, sprinkle a thick layer of rye flour on top before rising.
2. When the dough has risen, add the remaining 2½ cups flour, salt, and vegetable shortening. Mix well. Cover and set aside in a warm place to rise again until double, about 45 minutes. (If you use starter dough, the second rising could take an hour or more to begin.)
3. Place in 2 small greased loaf pans. Cover and let rise again, about 45 minutes. Preheat oven to 375 degrees F. Brush beaten egg over dough and bake for 40 minutes or until brown.

MAKES 2 LOAVES.

Traditional Rye Bread

3½ cups apple cider
2 tablespoons caraway seeds
5½ cups coarse whole grain rye flour
1 cup sourdough starter (equal parts water and bread flour)
1 (¼-ounce) package dry yeast
1 teaspoon salt
2½ cups all-purpose flour

1. Bring 3 cups apple cider and the caraway seeds to a boil. Add 3 cups rye flour. Mix well. Let mixture cool.
2. Add 1 cup active sourdough starter. Mix well to form a heavy porridge-like texture. Sprinkle ½ cup rye flour. Do not stir.
3. Cover the bowl. Wrap entire bowl with a cloth or blanket. Set aside in a warm, draft-free place for up to 24 hours for correct sourness.
4. Dissolve the yeast in the remaining ½ cup warm apple cider by letting it stand for 5 minutes. Gradually add the salt, all-purpose flour, and the remaining 2 cups rye flour. Knead with an electric mixer. Add more rye flour if necessary. The dough should remain firm and not get too wet.
5. Divide the dough in 2 loaves on a greased surface using wet hands. Place the loaves into 2 greased 8 × 4-inch loaf pans. Cover with a clean, damp dish towel and let rise in a warm, draft-free place until doubled, 1 to 2 hours.
6. Preheat oven to 400 degrees F. Bake for 15 minutes. Turn down the heat to 350 degrees F and continue to bake for an additional hour. Remove bread from pans and set to cool.

MAKES 2 LOAVES.

Baltic Bread
Baltmaize

½ (¼-ounce) package dry yeast
2 cups whole milk
about 5 cups all-purpose flour plus extra for kneading
3 tablespoons butter
1 tablespoon sugar
pinch of salt

1. Dissolve yeast in a little warm water by letting it stand for 5 minutes. Mix with all ingredients. Knead dough. Cover with a damp, clean dish towel and set aside in a warm, draft-free place (about 80 degrees F) to rise until doubled, 1 to 2 hours. (If the room is cold, place pan of covered dough on rack over a large pan of hot, steaming water.)
2. Preheat oven to 425 degrees F. Place dough in 2 small greased loaf pans. Bake until brown or about 50 minutes.

Delicious with honey or homemade preserves.

MAKES 2 SMALL LOAVES.

In the old days, bread was treated with great respect. If a piece of bread fell on the floor, children were taught to kiss it in apology.

Every Latvian household has its own recipe for *pīrāgi*, or Latvian dumplings. I found it impossible to decide which was best. The origin of these tasty stuffed dumplings is uncertain, and many of Latvia's Russians claim them as Russian.

Historically Latvia has always had ties to Russia. Today the enormous influx of Russian workers during Soviet times has left 34% of Latvia's population Russian. Latvians are, however, reclaiming Latvia as their own. In May 1995, for example, Latvian revelers celebrated the fifth anniversary of Latvia's declaration of independence by blowing up a 19-story tower on the radar site in Russian military town, Skrunda. The town is home to the USSR's most westerly early-warning radar station, which was under Russian control until last year. The annual concert Rock against Militarism marks the event.

Although most memories of Russia belong to Soviet times and are not complimentary, Russia's ties with Latvia brought more than just Soviet block buildings. If these dumplings are indeed originally Russian, they might be considered one of the positive remnants of Russian influence. I've included several different recipes here. The *pīrāgi* are best when eaten the day they are baked, or the day after.

Pīrāgi Dough I

Makes 10 to 20 *pīrāgi*.

2 cups flour
1 cup + 2 tablespoons (2¼ sticks) butter
salt
3 tablespoons water

1. Mix the flour and butter with a little salt. Add water. Knead the mixture well. Let stand for about an hour.
2. Shape and fill as directed below.

Pīrāgi Dough II

Makes 8 to 12 *pīrāgi*.

¼ cup water
salt
1 egg
1 cup all-purpose flour (plus about ¼ cup for kneading)
1 teaspoon lemon juice or lemon sugar

1. Mix water, salt, egg, flour, and lemon juice together. Knead the mixture well.
2. Shape and fill as directed below.

Pīrāgi Dough III

Makes 60 to 80 *pīrāgi*.

½ cup warm water
2 teaspoons sugar
2 (¼-ounce each) packages dry yeast
2 cups whole milk, scaled
½ cup oil
2 tablespoons sugar
2 teaspoons salt
2 eggs, lightly beaten
½ cup sour cream
6 cups all-purpose flour

1. Mix sugar and water and sprinkle yeast on top. Set aside in a warm place for 10 to 15 minutes or until it has bubbled up to about twice the size. Prepare yeast by mixing all the ingredients.
2. Place scalded milk, oil, sugar, and salt in a large mixing bowl and mix well. Set aside to cool.
3. In a separate bowl, mix eggs and sour cream. When milk has cooled slightly, add egg mixture.
4. Add yeast mixture and 2 cups flour. Beat thoroughly with electric mixer. Add another cup of flour and continue beating.
5. Continue mixing with a spoon and add all but a few tablespoons of the remaining 3 cups flour. Remove dough from bowl and knead on a lightly floured surface. Knead hard for about 5 minutes.
6. Place dough in a clean bowl that has been lightly coated with oil. Cover the bowl with a clean, damp dish towel and set aside to rise in a warm, draft-free place, about 1 to 2 hours.
7. Shape and fill as directed below.

Pīrāgi Dough IV

Makes 20 to 30 *pīrāgi*.

1 (¼-ounce) package dry yeast
dried lemon peel, raisins, cardamom (optional)
½ cup fat, melted or well-beaten
2¾ cups wheat flour (plus about ¾ cup for kneading)
1 cup warm milk
1 teaspoon salt
½ cup sugar
1 or 2 eggs (optional)

1. Mix yeast with ¼ cup warm water in a bowl. Set aside for 5 minutes to dissolve. Add lemon peel, raisins, and cardamom if desired. Add melted fat (which should be warm, not hot).
2. Add wheat flour and mix well.
3. Add milk to mixture and mix from center. Add salt and sugar. (For sweeter dough, add more sugar. You may also add 1 or 2 eggs if desired.) Place dough in a clean bowl that has been lightly coated with oil and cover the bowl with a clean, damp dish towel. Set aside to let the dough rise in a warm, draft-free place until doubled in size, 1 to 2 hours.
4. After the dough has risen, knead it well. Cover and let rise again until doubled, about 45 minutes. Knead well again. Make sure that you have enough flour on hand so that dough doesn't stick to your hands.
5. Shape and fill as directed below.

TRADITIONAL BACON FILLING:

oil for frying
2 pounds lean bacon, diced fine
1 medium onion, diced fine
pepper
salt

1. Heat oil and fry bacon and onion together.
2. Add salt and pepper to taste. Let cool in refrigerator.

TRADITIONAL CABBAGE FILLING:

oil for frying
2 pounds white cabbage, finely chopped
2 or 3 large onions, finely chopped
1 tablespoon salt
2 eggs, hard-boiled

1. Heat the oil in a frying pan and add cabbage and onions. Add salt to taste. Cook until cabbage is soft. Let cool.
2. Add hard-boiled eggs. Mix well.

Other popular fillings are sauerkraut and rice mixed with hard-boiled eggs or ground beef.

Shaping *pīrāgi:*

1. Preheat oven to 400 degrees F.
2. Shape into two long round rolls. Cut 1-inch pieces from each roll. Flatten each piece so that you can place about 1 teaspoon of filling onto each piece. Fold edges around filling and pinch ends together. Brush each pīrāgi with a lightly beaten egg and pierce with a fork a few times.
3. Bake on greased baking sheets for 10 to 15 minutes or until brown.

Pērkons brauca pa jūriņu
Putošā laiviņā.
Brauc, Pērkon, Vidzemē
Apraudzīt Vidzemītes:
Vidzemnieki gauži lūdz-
Miežiem asni novītuši.

Perkons sails over the sea
In a foamy boat.
Sail, Perkons, to Vidzeme,
Come to see how it's faring:
The Vidzeme people are
    earnestly praying,
For the barley sprouts have
    wilted.

—Latvian folk song

Cabbage Bread

¾ head cabbage
¾ to 1 pound smoked bacon
oil for frying
1 onion, cut in small pieces
salt
pepper
paprika
caraway (optional)
3 eggs, hard-boiled and cut in small pieces
Pīrāgi Dough IV (without optional ingredients; page 45)
1 egg, beaten

1. To make filling, chop cabbage. Fry bacon. Cut into small pieces. Stew cabbage with oil, onion, and bacon. Add salt, pepper, and paprika to taste. If desired, add caraway as well.
2. Add hard-boiled eggs to mixture. Let mixture cool.
3. Roll dough out well. Divide into two parts. Roll out one part until it is about ½ inch thick. Place in a 9 × 9-inch greased baking dish. Cover with a clean, damp dish towel and let rise 1 to 2 hours. Set aside other half to rise at the same time.
4. After the dough in the baking dish has risen, preheat oven to 425 degrees F. Place the cabbage mixture on top of the dough and cover it with the other layer.
5. Brush beaten egg on top of dough and bake for about 30 minutes or until light brown.

Serve with broth or salad.

MAKES 8 TO 10 SERVINGS.

Lād man ļaudis, buŗ man ļaudis,	People curse me, people bewitch me.
Nevar mani izpostīt:	They cannot destroy me:
Dieviņš taisa zelta sētu	Dievs raises a gold fence
Apkārt manu augumiņu.	All around my body.

—Latvian folk song

The Song Father, also known as Dievs, in Dainu Kalns.

Ham *Pīrāgi*

Pīrāgi Dough II (page 43)
1 to 1½ cups thinly sliced ham
a few tablespoons mustard
1 egg, beaten

1. Combine the dough ingredients and knead well. Refrigerate dough for about 30 minutes. Remove and cut in 2 × 2-inch squares.
2. Preheat oven to 425 degrees F. Place one piece of thinly sliced ham in the middle of each square. Spread mustard on ham. From one end of square, begin rolling dough around ham to form roll.
3. Brush beaten egg on top. Sprinkle pan with water. Bake for 10 to 15 minutes.

MAKES 8 TO 12 *pīrāgi*.

ANCIENT LATVIAN CUSTOM: Since ancient times Latvians have enjoyed *pirts,* or bathhouses, which are similar to steam-houses. Most farms had their own bathhouse where bathers sat on benches and swatted themselves with birch twigs to open up their pores and aid circulation. In the winter, they rubbed down with snow in between baths. Our friend Veronica, who was born in a *pirt,* explained that Latvian mothers often gave birth to their children in these clean, "pure" bathhouses as well.

Beef *Pīrāgi*

············

Pīrāgi Dough II (page 43)
¼ pound ground beef
1 onion, chopped
salt
pepper
1 egg, beaten

1. Prepare the dough and refrigerate for 30 minutes.
2. Brown the ground beef with onion. Drain fat. Season to taste with salt and pepper.
3. Take dough from refrigerator. Roll out dough until thin. Make sure the dough is not so thin that you see holes. Cut into rectangles, about 3 × 1½-inches. Brush with beaten egg.
4. Preheat oven to 425 degrees F. Pile small amount of beef in center. Fold opposite corners together and press ends together to make dumplings. Brush with beaten egg. Bake for 10 to 15 minutes until browned.

MAKES 8 TO 12 *pīrāgi.*

Hot Dog *Pīrāgi*

Pīrāgi Dough II (page 43)
10 small hot dogs
mustard (optional)

1. Prepare the dough and refrigerate for 30 minutes.
2. Slice and halve hot dogs.
3. Take dough from refrigerator, and roll out well. Slice into long strips.
4. Preheat oven to 425 degrees F.
5. Add mustard to inside of hot-dog slice. Wrap dogs in dough. Add more mustard on top if you wish. Bake for 10 to 15 minutes until done.

MAKES 8 TO 12 *pīrāgi*.

According to legend, the Devil roamed the earth and tempted girls with his bucket full of bright colors. By the time he arrived in Latvia, however, he was so tired that he fell asleep. Girls from all over the country ran to color their skirts with the Devil's paints. Some managed to color their skirts entirely, while others only managed a narrow red trim.

So originated the Latvian national costumes. Today there are hundreds of different national costumes worn for special occasions throughout the year. Women wear dark gray or brown skirts patterned according to their region. Embroidered blouses are adorned with silver brooches. Men wear trousers with a woven, woolen belt.

Smoked Bacon *Pīrāgi*

⅔ cup (1¼ sticks) butter or margarine
½ to ¾ cup heavy cream
1 egg yolk
1 tablespoon rum or vodka
½ to 1 cup wheat flour
¼ pound cooked smoked bacon
1 egg, beaten

1. Melt butter and slowly add cream.
2. Mix the yolk with the rum. Add to cream. Add enough wheat flour to separate the dough from the spoon. The dough should still be thick enough to roll out. Refrigerate overnight.
3. The next day, roll the dough into a thin layer. Preheat oven to 425 degrees F. Cut half moon shapes from the dough. Place bacon on upper half of the half moon. Cover with the lower half and press the edges together.
4. Brush with beaten egg and pierce with a fork. Bake until brown, 15 to 20 minutes.

MAKES 6 TO 8 SERVINGS.

Soups
and
Porridges

Laima
Fate

Laima, the Goddess of Fate, determines the fortunes of new-born babies. She is depicted most often in the branches of a linden tree. Laima lives under the threshold and is not to be disturbed by lingering over it. Traditionally white hens are offered to secure favor with her.

Laima's symbol, which is seen on babies' cribs and a new mother's clothing, represents the needles of a fir branch.

Kādu Laim mūžu lika
Tāds bij manim jādzīvo
Es nevaru pāri kāpti
Par Laimiņas likumiņu.

As Laima cast my life
So must I live it.
I cannot go counter
To dear Laima's decree.

Uldis Jaunzems-Petersons, who taught me how to make the following soup, concocted his first milk soup at the age of three. This notable feat demonstrates the strong role milk soups play in Latvian kitchens. The soups are quite delicious.

Traditionally milk was used to make porridge, and barley and rye porridges were the most popular. In the 19th century, when potatoes began to be produced widely throughout Latvia, peasants added potatoes to the porridge. Most recipes called to add barley flour to a pot of boiled potatoes until a thick porridge formed. Milk was added before serving.

Fish has always been a staple in the Latvian diet, and it quickly became a popular component of milk soup as well. Most fish milk soups are cooked with pepper, saffron, butter, eggs, onions, salt, and sap. One 18th-century recipe for sprat soup required the cook to add sprats (also known as Baltic pilchards) to a pot of boiling sliced potatoes. Milk was added before serving, and the soup was seasoned with salt and chives. Rarely has meat been an ingredient of milk soup, although smoked mutton was occasionally boiled with groats and vegetables, with milk added before serving. Some peasants also used to make a milk soup when they slaughtered a pig. The pig's blood was cooked with milk, cooled, and then boiled in water. The coagulated blood was then cut, roasted in fat for about 20 minutes, and seasoned with salt, pepper, and mustard. To finish, the pieces were boiled again with sweet milk.

By the early 1900s, rural Latvians were using flour milk porridge for ritual functions. In Latgale, for example, the first pasturing and ploughing were always celebrated with porridge; herdsmen and ploughmen were the first served on these occasions. In those days flour porridge was cooked with water before adding milk. Occasionally flour was mixed with cold water and added to boiling milk.

Milk Soup with Vegetables

This delicious milk soup is one of the simplest and most popular today. You may substitute other fresh or frozen vegetables for the ones listed.

1 medium head cauliflower, cut in small pieces
4 leeks, diced
2 cups chopped carrots (about 4 medium carrots)
2 cups whole milk
¼ cup butter
pepper
salt

1. Boil cauliflower, leeks, and carrots in 2 cups water.
2. Add milk. Bring to boil again.
3. Add butter. Add pepper and salt to taste. Simmer for 10 minutes.

MAKES 4 TO 6 SERVINGS.

Milk Fish Soup

2 pounds any type fresh fish
1 tablespoon butter
1 onion, chopped
3 carrots, chopped
5 tablespoons fresh dill, plus additional for garnish
5 peppercorns
1 bay leaf
3 or 4 potatoes, peeled and chopped
about 3 cups milk
sour cream
lemon slices
chives

1. Clean fish without removing the head.
2. In a pot of water, add butter, onion, carrots, dill, peppercorns, and bay leaf and set to boil. Simmer until carrots are tender. Add whole fish and simmer until fish is tender. Remove from heat. Set fish aside to cool.
3. Strain broth. (Return boiled carrots to broth if desired.) Add potatoes and cook until tender.
4. Carefully scrape skin off fish. Lift meat away from the bones. Return fish without bones to pot.
5. Add milk. Spoon a teaspoon sour cream, a lemon slice, chives, and dill to each serving bowl. Add soup and serve immediately.

MAKES 6 TO 8 SERVINGS.

Cold Vegetable Soup

1 carrot, cut in small pieces
¼ head cauliflower, cut in small pieces
¼ cup fresh peas
¼ cup chopped cucumber
½ egg, hard-boiled and cut in small pieces
1 to 5 tablespoons sour cream
1 teaspoon sugar
juice from 1 lemon
salt
chives
parsley
dill

1. Add carrot, cauliflower, and peas to 4 to 5 cups boiling water. Boil 6 to 10 minutes or until vegetables are crispy-soft.
2. After vegetables are cooked, remove the pot of boiled vegetables from heat and refrigerate.
3. When cold, add cucumber, egg, sour cream, sugar, and lemon juice. Add salt, chives, parsley, and dill to taste.

MAKES 3 TO 4 SERVINGS.

Vegetarian Soup

1 cup chopped carrots (about 2 medium carrots)
about 2 cups (½ head) cauliflower, cut in small pieces
½ onion, chopped fine
1 tablespoon diced leek
2 tablespoons chopped fresh parsley
1 egg yolk
3 tablespoons heavy cream
dill
salt

1. Add carrots, cauliflower, onion, leek, and parsley to about 5 cups
   boiling water. Boil until vegetables are soft, 4 to 8 minutes.
2. Mix egg yolk with cream. Add to soup. Mix well. Add dill and
   salt to taste.

MAKES 4 TO 6 SERVINGS.

ANCIENT LATVIAN BELIEF: Latvian farmers welcome white storks, which are said to bring luck. Some farmers even attempt to lure storks to their farms by placing a cart wheel on a pole or in a tree in which the stork can build a nest. An estimated 6,000 to 7,000 storks arrive from Africa every April—six times as many as in all of Western Europe.

Pea Soup

1 pound dried peas
about 2 pounds pork hock or shoulder
1 large carrot, chopped
1 medium chopped onion
3 tablespoons barley
3 potatoes, diced

1. Wash peas, cover with water, and soak overnight.
2. Boil peas in the same water they soaked in. Add a few more cups water for soup. Add pork hock, carrot, onion, and barley. Simmer about 1½ hours.
3. Remove onion from mixture. Add diced potatoes and boil another 30 minutes.
4. Remove meat. Cut the meat and return it to the soup or serve it on rye bread as a side dish.

MAKES 6 TO 10 SERVINGS.

ANCIENT LATVIAN BELIEF: When the sun shines through the rain, a wedding is underway in the netherworld.

Mousse with Dumplings

5½ cups whole milk
2 eggs, separated
2 tablespoons wheat flour
½ teaspoon salt
sugar
cinnamon

1. Bring 4½ cups milk and a pinch of salt to a boil.
2. In a bowl, make dough by mixing 1 cup milk, 2 egg yolks, and wheat flour.
3. Beat egg whites until stiff. Add to dough.
4. Slowly pour the dough into the boiling milk. With a wooden spoon, carefully lift the dough from the milk. It will tear into pieces and form dumplings. Continue to boil the soup for 5 minutes.
5. Add salt. Add sugar and cinnamon for a sweet soup.

Serve hot.

VARIATION: Add a pinch more salt rather than sugar and cinnamon to serve as a salted soup.

MAKES 4 SERVINGS.

Meatball Soup
·····························
Frikadelu zupa

You may eliminate the beef chops and use 12 cups prepared beef broth instead of making your own; proceed to step 4.

½ pound beef chops
1 cup soft white bread crumbs (not toasted)
½ pound ground beef
2 eggs
salt
pepper
3 raw potatoes, peeled and chopped into small pieces
2½ cups chopped carrots (about 5 medium carrots)
¼ cup finely chopped fresh chives
¼ cup finely chopped fresh parsley

BROTH:
1. Run warm water over chops to loosen meat.
2. Pull meat from bone in small pieces and place meat pieces and bone in 12 cups water over low heat. Bring to a boil. Reduce the heat and cover. Let simmer for about 45 minutes or until meat is cooked through.
3. Remove the meat and bone. Strain the broth. Set aside over low heat. (The recipe on page 139 "Come back again" uses leftover meat.)

SOUP:

4. Mix together bread crumbs, ground beef, and 2 eggs. Add salt and pepper to taste. Set aside.
5. Add chopped potatoes to broth and bring to boil again. Reduce heat. After potatoes are cooked, add carrots. Let simmer about 10 minutes.
6. With wet, cold hands, make small meatballs from ground beef mixture. Add immediately to broth.
7. Add some of the chives and more salt and pepper if necessary. Bring to a boil. Serve when meatballs are cooked (about 30 minutes).

Garnish with parsley and chives.

MAKES 8 TO 10 SERVINGS.

There are as many different recipes for beet soup as there are for pīrāgi. Following are several different ones:

Traditional Beet Soup

8 cups beef stock
½ medium head of cabbage, finely shredded
3 medium potatoes, cut into 1-inch cubes
1 large red beet, shredded
1 tablespoon red-wine vinegar
3½ tablespoons bacon fat
2 teaspoons sugar
2 peeled tomatoes, chopped
2 tablespoons (¼ stick) butter
2 medium onions, finely chopped
1 carrot, sliced
1½ parsnips, chopped
6 peppercorns
3 bay leaves
1 clove garlic, peeled and chopped
chopped fresh parsley
sour cream

1. Bring the beef stock to a boil in a large soup pot. Add cabbage and potatoes and let simmer for 15 minutes.

2. Mix the beet, vinegar, 1½ teaspoons of the bacon fat, sugar, and tomatoes in a separate covered saucepan and cook over low heat about 5 minutes. Set aside. In a separate pan, melt the butter and add the onions, carrot, and parsnip. Cover and stew for 15 to 20 minutes.

3. Add both mixtures to the large soup pot. Add peppercorns and bay leaves. Let simmer another 10 minutes.

4. Add the garlic, the remaining 3 tablespoons bacon fat, and the chopped parsley. Then turn the heat down very low and cover the pot slightly. Let simmer for 4 to 5 hours. Allow to cool overnight. Reheat to serve.

5. Garnish with sour cream.

MAKES 10 TO 12 SERVINGS.

Beet Soup with Chicken

4 chicken breasts or one whole chicken (5 to 6 pounds)
2 large red beets
2½ cups chopped carrots (about 5 medium carrots)
oil for frying
1 medium onion, chopped
salt
pepper
1½ cups chopped sweet pickles (about 12 small pickles)
5 potatoes, peeled and cut in small pieces
1 garlic clove, crushed
1 cup chopped green onions
½ cup sour cream
1 cup chopped fresh parsley

BROTH:
1. Bring chicken to a boil in 8 to 10 cups water. Reduce heat and simmer until cooked.
2. Remove the chicken and excess fat. Set chicken aside. Strain the broth. Set aside over low heat.

SOUP:

3. Boil unpeeled beets or bake in oven until soft. Peel and grate coarsely.
4. Sauté carrots in oil for about 15 minutes over low heat. Remove when cooked but still slightly crisp. Set aside.
5. Sauté onion. Set aside.
6. Cut cooked chicken into small pieces. In a covered frying pan, fry in oil over medium to high heat with salt and pepper until slightly brown. (Add more seasonings if desired.) Stir occasionally.
7. Place chicken back in broth, adding about 3 cups water. Add beets, sautéed carrots, and onions. Bring to a boil.
8. Add pickles and let simmer about 15 minutes.
9. Add chopped potatoes.
10. Sauté garlic in oil and add to soup. Simmer for about 20 minutes, adding more water if necessary. Add green onions.
11. Add salt and pepper to taste.

Serve with a dollop of sour cream. Garnish with parsley.

MAKES 6 TO 8 SERVINGS.

Beet Soup with Beef

BROTH:
¾ pound beef bones
1 stalk celery, diced
2 carrots, diced
1 bunch parsley, chopped
1 onion, cut in small pieces
1 pound red beets, peeled and grated

1. Bring the beef bones and 5 cups cold water to a boil. Boil about 20 minutes.
2. Add celery, carrots, parsley, onion, and beets. Boil for about 30 minutes. Strain the broth. Set aside over low heat.

SOUP:
1 pound red beets
1 tablespoon wheat flour
1 tablespoon sour cream
1 tablespoon wine vinegar
salt

3. In a covered pot, bring the beets to a boil. Cook until soft. Set aside beets and water.
4. Mix wheat flour and sour cream. Add to broth to thicken. Boil for 5 minutes. Add the juice from the cooked beets.
5. Add vinegar. Add salt slowly to taste.

Serve with baked potatoes, patties with salted pork fat (see page 141), or toasted white bread with cheese. Garnish with the fat from roasted meat or meat drippings.

MAKES 6 TO 8 SERVINGS.

Beet Soup with Beef Short Ribs

1 pound boneless beef short ribs
1 tablespoon salt
1 bay leaf
1 onion, chopped fine
5 peppercorns
5 medium beets, cooked and grated
2 stalks celery, cut in small pieces
1 bunch fresh parsley, chopped fine
1½ cups chopped carrots (about 3 medium carrots)
8 cups chopped white cabbage (about 1 head)
2½ cups chopped tomatoes (about 3 tomatoes)
1 teaspoon dill
½ cup sour cream
lemon juice

1. Cover the meat with water in a saucepan and bring water to a boil. Add salt, bay leaf, onion, and peppercorns. Simmer until meat is cooked, about 45 minutes.
2. Add beets, celery, parsley, carrots, cabbage, tomatoes, and dill.
3. Boil about 15 more minutes or until cabbage is soft. Before serving, add sour cream and lemon juice for a slightly sour taste.

MAKES 8 TO 10 SERVINGS.

Cheese Soup

4 potatoes, peeled and cubed
2 carrots, peeled and cut in small pieces
1 medium onion, cut in small pieces
1 green pepper, diced
chives
salt
pepper
12 ounces any very soft, mild white cheese, shredded
chopped fresh parsley

1. Bring potatoes and carrots to a boil. When they are almost cooked, add onions and green pepper. Add chives, salt, and pepper to taste.
2. After the vegetables are cooked, stir the soup carefully and add cheese a little at a time. Continue to stir until soup begins to boil.

Garnish with parsley.

MAKES 4 TO 5 SERVINGS.

*The owner of the House of Cats in Old Riga com-
missioned the cats which perch atop the building
after his membership in the Merchant's Guild
across the street was declined. To spite the
Guild's members, he ordered the cats to be posi-
tioned with their tails facing the Guild. Taking
this as the insult it was meant to be, members
agreed to admit him into the Guild and the cats
were turned around.*

Sorrel Soup I

....

1 pound meaty beef bones
2 cups chopped carrots (about 4 carrots)
3 cups chopped new potatoes (about 5 small potatoes)
1 cup finely chopped sorrel
6 green onions, chopped fine
2 tablespoons finely chopped fresh dill
2 tablespoons finely chopped fresh chives
salt
pepper
2 eggs, hard-boiled and cut in small pieces
½ cup sour cream

BROTH:

1. Boil beef bones in 8 to 10 cups water for about an hour, or until a good broth is formed and some of the meat has fallen off the bones.
2. Remove bones from broth. Let simmer.

SOUP:

3. Add chopped carrots and potatoes to broth. Let simmer for about 30 minutes or until vegetables are cooked.
4. Add sorrel. Let simmer about 10 minutes.
5. Add green onions, dill, and chives. Add salt and pepper to taste.

To serve, place 1 to 2 tablespoons hard-boiled egg in the bottom of each soup bowl. Pour soup into bowl. Serve with a dollop of sour cream.

MAKES 6 TO 8 SERVINGS.

Sorrel Soup II

If you have no sorrel on hand, mix 1 additional cup spinach with a teaspoon of lemon juice.

1 pound meaty beef bones
½ cup chopped sorrel
½ cup chopped spinach
2 tablespoons wheat flour
½ cup sour cream
salt
2 eggs, hard-boiled

1. Make broth using beef bones, see step 1 of previous recipe.
2. Add chopped sorrel mixed with spinach to broth.
3. Mix the wheat flour with sour cream. In a separate pot, place the flour and sour cream over medium heat.
4. When hot, add a pinch of salt to flour mixture and pour into broth.

To serve, cut the boiled eggs in quarters and place some in each bowl. Pour soup into bowls.

MAKES 6 TO 8 SERVINGS.

Pēc goda, pēc varas, pēc mantas
Bez atpūtas ļautiņi skrien,
Tie dzenās, tie cīnas, tie pūlas,
Ar rūpēm tie kapenēs lien.

Gan lauri tiem kapenes pušķo,
Gan varoņu dziesmās tos min, —
Ne greznumu mana, ne dziesmas,
Ko miroņu tumsība tin.

For glory, for power, for riches
Men ceaselessly labor in vain,
They strive and they chase and they struggle,
Then crawl with their cares to the grave.

Though their graves may be covered with laurel,
And their lives praised by every man's breath,
No pomp and no singing can banish
The darkness that comes with their death.

—Eduards Veidenbaums (1867-1892), Latvian poet

Sauerkraut Soup

5 cups broth (see recipe page 70)
2 cups chopped sauerkraut
½ cup sour cream
salt
6 small potatoes, chopped and boiled or sautéed

1. Bring broth to a boil.
2. Add sauerkraut and boil until soft, 20 to 30 minutes.
3. Add sour cream. Add salt to taste.
4. Before serving, add potatoes.

MAKES 5 TO 6 SERVINGS.

ANCIENT LATVIAN BELIEF: If you sit at the corner of a table you won't get married for seven years.

Pike and Potato Soup

You may eliminate the firm-fleshed fish and use 4 to 5 cups prepared fish stock instead of making your own; proceed to step 3.

BROTH:
1 firm-fleshed fish or 1 to 2 pounds assorted fish
2 tablespoons chopped fresh parsley
½ onion, chopped fine
2 cups chopped potatoes

1. To make boning easier, soak the firm-fleshed fish in hot water for a short time. Then cut off the head and remove the bones.
2. Boil fish in 4 to 5 cups water for 45 minutes to 1 hour or until fish is cooked. Strain broth in a sieve.
3. Add parsley, onions, and potatoes. Let simmer.

SOUP:
2 pike fillets
salt
¾ tablespoon butter
dill

4. In a separate pot, boil pike fillets until cooked. (They should turn white.) Cut into pieces.
5. Add to broth. Add salt to taste.

Garnish with butter and dill before serving.

MAKES 3 TO 4 SERVINGS.

Cod Ball Soup

SOUP:

6 cups fish bouillon (see page 78 or use prepared broth)
4 small carrots, cut in small pieces
2 onions, chopped
7 potatoes, peeled and cut in small pieces
parsley
salt
pepper
dill

1. Bring fish bouillon to a boil. Add carrots, onions, potatoes, and parsley.
2. Bring to a boil again. Add salt, pepper, and dill to taste.

FISH BALLS:

1 pound cod fillet
2 thick slices white bread
2 tablespoons condensed milk
1 egg, beaten
salt
pepper

3. Grind cod fillet with white bread, milk, egg, salt, and pepper in a meat grinder or food processor. With cold, wet hands, form fish balls from mixture.
4. Add to broth. Let simmer until fish is cooked, about an hour.

MAKES 4 TO 5 SERVINGS.

Sculpture in Cēsis castle.

The pride of Latvia's northeastern Vidzeme region is Cēsis, host to summer open-air operas, a medieval knights' festival, and a rollicking annual beer festival in celebration of Cēsis beer, which dates to 1590. The city was spared much of the industrialization and Russification suffered by other provincial towns while under Soviet rule, and today it retains much of its medieval charm. Cēsis is steeped in history, culture, and the traditions of the former Livonian nationalities. The Knights of the Sword, later the Livonian Order, built the local castle, the focal point of the town, in 1206 as a base for further conquests in northern Latvia and southern Estonia. It is also the home of the Latvian flag. As legend goes, Namejs the king of the Latgals tribe was wounded at the Cēsis castle in 1272 and lay dying on a white cloth. The cloth turned red with blood on either side of the dying king but remained white across the middle where he lay. From this cloth came the maroon-white-maroon Latvian flag, which was eventually instituted in 1280.

After the defeat of the Knights of the Sword in the Battle of Saule in 1236, Hermann Balke, the first Master of the Livonian Order, chose Cēsis as his residence, and the castle remained the residence of the Masters of the Livonian Order until 1561. The town was soon an important administrative center of the Livonian Church State; it was the only city in ancient Livonia besides Rīga to coin its own money.

Not surprisingly, the Livonian territories' proximity to western Europe has tempted the Russians throughout the centuries. Czar Ivan IV (the Terrible), for example, was determined to control the Livonian territories and attacked repeatedly. The Cēsis region in particular suffered enormous atrocities. Ivan and his Russian hordes mutilated and roasted alive the defenders of the castle, burned farm houses, ravaged fields, and slaughtered so much livestock that the remaining peasants had to pull the plows. The task of reconstruction was monumental. One traveler noted that he did not hear a rooster crow or a dog bark during a journey through the region.

Around the end of the 16th century, the original castle premises were adjusted to accommodate the Cēsis castle estate, or New Castle, which in 1777 became the property of Count Carl Eberhard von Sievers, a soldier of the Imperial Russian Army. He built his residence quarters on the castle's east end. The front yard was enclosed by a granary and a stablecoach house, which currently houses an exhibition center for local artists. Along the granary wall opposite is a poignant memorial to those who suffered under Communist terrorism.

Cēsis attracted attention again as the site of a decisive war during Latvia's War of National Liberation (1918–1920), when the victory against the Germans in the region eventually drove them out of Latvia. A statue of a small boy holding a gun, a memorial to a regiment of schoolboys who fought during the war, stands on Beazaines iela. After independence was won, the Cēsis Manor was divided under the agrarian reform in 1921, and the central buildings were given to the 8th Daugavpils Regiment of the Latvian Army. Four years later, the Cēsis Association of Museums founded the Cēsis Museum of History here.

I joined thousands of Latvians on the hillside opposite the castle one June evening to hear Puccini's *Turandot*, which was staged at the castle. The opera, complete with a live orchestra and ornate costumes, ended with an impressive display of fireworks. A monument to Alfreds Kalnins (1879–1951), who composed the first Latvian national opera "Banuta," stands on a street nearby.

Also of interest is the old farmhouse Betes just outside town, which has been used as a gallery and workshop by pottery craftspeople from all over Latvia since the country's independence. Newly married couples often visit to mold a pot, which symbolizes the start of their lives together.

Here is a recipe from the Vidzeme region.

Vidzeme Sour Porridge

¼ cup finely ground barley groats
⅔ cup whole milk
salt
½ cup sour milk
1 tablespoon sour cream

1. Bring groats to a boil in 1 to 1¼ cups water. Reduce the heat to low and cook, covered, until the barley is tender and water is absorbed, about 45 minutes.
2. Add whole milk and salt and bring to a boil again.
3. Add sour milk and boil again. When a thin skin forms, the porridge is ready. Serve hot with sour cream immediately or refrigerate for 2 days and serve cold with sour cream.

MAKES 2 TO 3 SERVINGS.

Pērkons brauca pa jūriņu,
Lietiņš lija jūriņā.
Arājs lūdza Pērkonīti:
Brauc, Pērkoni, šai zemē,
Brauc, Pērkoni, šai zemē,
Miežam asni novītuši!

Thunder rode across the sea.
It rained into the sea.
The peasant praying to
  Thunder called:
"Come, Thunder, to this land,
Come, Thunder, to this land,
For here the barley shoots are
  withering!"

—Latvian folk song

In ancient Courland, the western region of Latvia and today's Kurzeme, it was customary to have a large pot of porridge on hand for a refreshment, especially in the summer months. The kingdom of Courland was home to the seafaring Cours, once the most powerful Baltic people. By 1230, however, the Livonian knights of Germany, determined to Christianize the pagan Baltics, were a threat to the Cours. Although Cours leader Lamekins was baptized as a Christian in an effort to keep the knights at bay, the Germans eventually took over Courland in 1267. The Cours as a people disappeared until 1561, when the Livonian state collapsed under Ivan the Terrible and the last master of the Livonian Order, Gotthard Kettler, salvaged Courland as his own personal fiefdom.

Over the next 200 years, the region was called the Duchy of Courland. Duke Jacob, its ruler from 1640 to 1682, renewed Courland's former seafaring reputation and developed a sizable navy, merchant fleet, and shipbuilding industry. His ship *The Coat of Arms of the Duchess of Courland* traveled to settle two faraway colonies—Tobago in the Caribbean and an island in the mouth of the Gambia River. Although the Gambia island was never settled, 2000 Latvians settled on Tobago in the 1650s, and Willem Mollens, the captain of the Duke's ship, renamed the island New Kurland. The new arrivals built a fort called Jekab-forts on the southwest corner of the island and gave Cour names to other towns and bays; one bay is still named Great Kurzeme after the Latvian region. The Duchy remained largely independent until Duke Jacob's son married into the Russian royal family in 1795 and Russia absorbed the region.

Following is a traditional Courland recipe. When in Rīga, I recommend you sample a few of the traditional Cour dishes offered at the Rozamunda in Old Rīga. This Old World restaurant also serves specialties adapted from the Caribbean dishes learned by the Latvians who traveled there.

≈≈⊛≈≈

Sour Barley Porridge

Skāba Putra

¼ cup finely ground cracked barley
pinch of salt
2 cups buttermilk
4 cups skim milk
⅓ cup sour cream

1. Mix barley, 1 to 1¼ cups water, and salt together in large pot.
2. While mixing, bring to a boil slowly over medium heat. Reduce heat to low and cook, covered, until the barley is tender and the water is absorbed, about 45 minutes. Set aside and cool until slightly warm.
3. Add buttermilk and milk. Consistency should be that of a thick soup. Store overnight (up to 12 hours) in a warm place so that the porridge sours.
4. Refrigerate for several days so that the porridge continues to ferment slightly. Add sour cream before serving.

If desired, serve with salted pork fat (or regular bacon) and sautéed onions.

MAKES 6 TO 7 SERVINGS.

When Jānis Borgs, renowned gourmet and practitioner of curative fasting, ended the highly publicized second-longest fast of his life, he left the hunger-strike tent in the center of Rīga and headed directly to the much-acclaimed Vincents restaurant at Elizabetes iela 19. But not for Prince Charles' favorite, the steamed shrimp dim sum and ostrich fillet, for which the restaurant is famous. Instead, friend and resident chef Mārtiņš Rītiņš is rumored to have prepared a bowl of this porridge for him. Easy on the stomach, the soup is a favorite of all ages and wallets.

Rye-Flour Porridge
Rudzu miltu biezputra

salt
3½ cups rye flour (substitute: wheat flour)

1. Boil 8 cups water with salt. Add flour in water and stir constantly with wooden spoon until porridge is ready to serve.
2. Serve with bacon and milk or buttermilk.

MAKES 8 TO 10 SERVINGS.

Pancakes, Egg Dishes, and Cheeses

Jumis
Fertility

Granaries throughout Latvia are decorated with two interlocked stems, Jumis' symbol of fertility. In ancient Latvia a festival in Jumis' honor was celebrated at harvest time.

ANCIENT LATVIAN BELIEF: If you kiss a loved one over the threshold, you'll never see him again.

Potato Pancakes

2 eggs, beaten
3 cups grated raw potatoes
¼ cup grated onion
1 teaspoon salt
½ teaspoon pepper
2 tablespoons all-purpose flour
butter or oil for frying

1. Mix eggs, potatoes, onions, salt, pepper, and flour together in food processor until smooth.
2. Fry mixture in butter or oil, using about 1 tablespoon batter per pancake.

Serve with sour cream or applesauce.

MAKES 10 TO 15 PANCAKES.

Mushroom-Filled Potato Pancakes

3 or 4 potatoes, boiled and peeled
½ cup all-purpose flour
2 eggs
salt
pepper
½ cup chopped mushrooms
1 cup chopped cauliflower
butter for frying
¾ cup chopped leeks
sour cream
parsley

1. Mash potatoes. Mix flour and eggs, add salt and pepper to taste. Mix together with potatoes until very creamy.
2. Fry mushrooms and cauliflower in a small amount of butter. When soft, add leeks. Mix well. Remove from heat.
3. Make pancakes from potato mixture. Place a small amount of the mushroom mixture in the center of each pancake. Close all sides of pancake to wrap mixture well. You may prefer to fry one side lightly before adding mushroom mixture.
4. Fry in medium-size frying pan until brown.

Serve immediately. Garnish with sour cream and parsley.

MAKES 10 TO 12 PANCAKES.

We draw strength from the earth.
Rich rye seed flows through us all.
We are a people for ploughing, not war.
We suck strength from the lap of the earth.

—Jānis Rainis (1865–1929), Latvian poet

ANCIENT LATVIAN BELIEF: It is bad luck to shake hands or accept gifts over the threshold.

☙❀❧

Rye-Flour Pancakes
....
Rudzu miltu plāceņi

2 pounds potatoes (about 7 potatoes)
1¾ cups whole milk
1 teaspoon salt
1 tablespoon sugar
4½ to 5 cups rye flour
3 (¼-ounce) packages dry yeast
½ cup Crisco or other vegetable shortening

COTTAGE CHEESE FILLING
Biezpiena masai

2 cups cottage cheese
½ pound smoked bacon
caraway seeds

1. Peel and grate potatoes. Press liquid from grated potatoes. Boil milk.
2. Add potatoes, salt, and sugar to milk. Mix well. Sift flour. Mix yeast with small amount of water. Add flour, yeast, and Crisco. Mix and leave to rise for 45 minutes.
3. Cut round pancakes (3 to 4 inches in diameter) from dough. Some Latvians, who are great believers in recycling, cut the ends off a large tin can and use the mouth of the can to make the pancake shapes, cookie-cutter style. Put pancakes into greased pan and let rise for 15 to 20 minutes.
4. Strain cottage cheese. Fry bacon slightly and mince strips. Mix cottage cheese, bacon, and caraway seeds. After the pancake dough rises, press an indention in the middle of each pancake

and spoon cottage cheese mixture onto the pancake. (Or you may mix cottage cheese with sugar and spoon over each pancake.) Fold dough edges to the middle covering all but a small part of the cottage cheese on each pancake.

5. Fry the pancakes in a medium-size skillet.

MAKES 20 TO 30 PANCAKES.

Peasant Omelet
Zemnieku omlete

4 boiled potatoes
oil for frying
2 leeks
8 eggs
salt
pepper
4 tomatoes

1. Peel and slice potatoes. Heat oil in a large skillet. Fry potato slices until they are golden brown on both sides.
2. Chop leeks and sprinkle half over fried potatoes.
3. Mix eggs, salt, and pepper well. Pour mixture over potatoes. Wait for omelet to turn a golden brown.
4. Slice tomato. Sprinkle omelet with the rest of the leeks and decorate with tomato slices.

Serve immediately.

MAKES 8 SERVINGS.

Ābeļkoka laivu daru,
Abi gali pazeltīti,
Dieva dēli jīrējiņi,
Saules meitu vizina.

A boat of apple tree I make,
Both ends are gilded.
The sons of Dievs are the rowers,
Taking the daughter of the Sun
for a row.

—Latvian folk song

Sculpture in Bastion Hill park.

Apple Pancakes

3 eggs, beaten
sugar
1½ cups milk
about 2 cups all-purpose flour
pinch of baking soda
salt
3 apples, peeled and grated
olive oil for frying

1. Mix beaten eggs with a small amount of sugar to taste.
2. Add milk to eggs and mix well. Add flour so that the dough is very thick but still liquidy.
3. Add baking soda, a little salt, and grated apples. Mix well.
4. Fry in olive oil in a medium-size hot frying pan, using about 1 tablespoon of batter per pancake.

MAKES 20 TO 30 PANCAKES.

Carrot and Apple Pancakes

1 apple, peeled and cored
2½ cups chopped carrots (about 5 carrots)
1 cup flour
2 eggs
salt
oil for frying

1. Cut apple into small pieces.
2. Mix carrots, apple, flour, eggs, and a pinch of salt.
3. Fry pancakes in oil, using about 1 large tablespoon of batter per pancake.

MAKES 6 TO 8 SERVINGS.

Farmer's Breakfast
··
Zemnieku Brokastis

1 large onion, chopped fine
oil for frying
12 ounces smoked bacon, cut in small pieces
½ cup chopped milk sausage (substitute: ham or baloney)
½ cup (1 stick) butter
6 potatoes, peeled and diced
salt
1¼ cups chopped cucumber (about 1 cucumber)
1½ cups chopped tomatoes (about 2 tomatoes)
pepper
4 eggs
2 cups whole milk
½ cup chopped fresh parsley
½ cup chopped fresh chives
1 cup chopped small pickles (about 8 pickles)

1. Sauté onion in oil in large frying pan.
2. Add bacon, stirring occasionally.
3. Add sausage. Let simmer about 5 minutes. Stir occasionally.
4. In a separate pan, melt butter. Fry diced potatoes in butter over medium to high heat until brown, stirring occasionally. Add salt to taste.
5. Add cucumbers to large frying pan. Mix well. Add tomatoes, salt, and pepper to large frying pan.
6. In a bowl, mix the eggs and milk. Add parsley and chives. Set aside.
7. Add fried potatoes to large frying pan. Mix well.
8. Add milk/egg mixture to large frying pan. Mix well. Add pickles. Let simmer about 5 to 10 minutes. Serve immediately.

MAKES 6 TO 8 SERVINGS.

Sweet Omelet

5 eggs
¾ cup heavy cream
oil for frying

1. Mix eggs with cream.
2. Fry egg mixture in oil, stirring gently.

Serve on toast.

MAKES 3 TO 5 SERVINGS.

LATVIAN LEGEND: It is said that at the turn of each century, the devil rears his head from the dark waters of the Daugava River and asks if Rīga is finished yet. If the answer is yes, the river will swallow the city. After eight centuries Rīga is still not finished.

Old Riga's Philharmonic Square

Eggs and Bread Ring

Olas maizes gredzenos

1 large loaf wheat bread, without crust
3 eggs, beaten
butter for frying
milk sausage, sliced about ¼ inch thick, as many as
    there are slices of bread (substitute: baloney or ham)
6 ounces cheddar cheese, grated (1½ cups)

1. Cut loaf into four or five slices about 1½ inches thick. Hollow out each piece to form a ring. Dip each ring in beaten eggs.
2. In a covered frying pan, fry bread rings in butter, flipping occasionally, until brown on both sides.
3. In a separate pan, fry meat slices in butter. When slightly fried, place a slice of sausage in the center of each bread ring so that it fits snugly into the hole in the middle of the bread.
4. Sprinkle grated cheese on top of the meat. Cover and fry in butter for about 15 minutes.

MAKES 4 TO 6 SERVINGS.

Home Cheese

Majas siers

4½ cups (about 36 ounces) farmer's cheese
5 egg yolks
18 tablespoons (2¼ sticks) butter
1 tablespoon caraway
salt

1. Strain cottage cheese through sieve or food mill.
2. Mix egg yolks, butter, caraway, and salt. Add the cottage cheese.
3. Press the moisture from the mixture.

Refrigerate for 48 hours.

MAKES 5 TO 6 SERVINGS.

ANCIENT LATVIAN CUSTOM: Flowers, which bring good luck and wealth, bedeck the chairs of birthday children and brides. It is customary to bring an odd-numbered bouquet to weddings and dinner parties. (Even numbers imply completion, and even-numbered bouquets are presented only at funerals.)

Pashka

3 cups (24 ounces) farmer's cheese
¾ cup heavy cream
3 egg yolks
1 cup granulated sugar
splash of vanilla
juice from 1 lemon
grated lemon peel
3 almonds, ground
raisins
almonds
cinnamon

1. Strain the cheese through a sieve or food mill. Mix with cream. Wrap the mixture in a cheesecloth and let the moisture run off through the cloth over about a 12-hour period.
2. Beat egg yolks with sugar until creamy.
3. Mix vanilla, lemon juice, dry lemon, and ground almonds. Mix with cheese mixture. Add yolks. Add raisins, sweet almonds, and cinnamon to preferred taste.
4. Wrap in cheesecloth again and press the moisture through the cloth. Place in a colander or heavy pot. Weigh down and let run off in refrigerator. The cheese will be ready in 2 to 3 days.

MAKES 8 TO 10 SERVINGS.

Potatoes

Auseklis
Morning star

Used as a sign of unity during many independence struggles, this guardian star protects its bearer from evil and misfortune.

Mēnestiņis zvaigznes skaita,
Vai ir visas vakarā.
Ira visas vakarā,
Auseklīša vien nevaid;
Auseklītis aiztecēja
Saules meitas lūkoties.

The moon counts the stars,
Are they all out at nightfall?
All the stars are there,
All except the morning star;
For the morning star has gone
To gaze at the daughters of
the sun.

—Latvian folk song

Potatoes with Cheese Sauce

···

4 large potatoes, peeled and sliced
¼ to ½ cup (½ to 1 stick) butter
½ cup oil
1 cup heavy cream
salt

1. Fry potatoes in butter and oil, adding butter until they are well-coated. Cover, stirring occasionally.
2. After about 15 minutes, add cream and salt. Cook for 30 to 45 minutes or until slightly brown, stirring occasionally.

CHEESE SAUCE

The Latvian cheese my friend Uldis used for this dish is very strong and very nearly took the paint off the walls of my apartment. Use a milder white cheese if desired.

3 cups whole milk
1 medium onion, chopped fine
oil
1½ cups sour cream
salt
pepper
½ cup chopped fresh parsley
1 cup grated Latvijas siers, or Latvian cheese
     (substitute: any strong white cheese)

3. Bring milk to a boil. Set aside.
4. Sauté onion in oil. Add sour cream and salt and pepper to taste. Let simmer about 3 minutes over medium heat. Add parsley and more salt and pepper if necessary.

5. Add cheese and cook until melted. Mix cheese mixture and milk together for sauce.

6. Pour cheese sauce over potatoes and let simmer, covered, about 10 minutes. Serve immediately.

MAKES 6 SERVINGS.

Vēl Laimīt man mūžiņ,	Laima, please determine my life,
Vēl liepā, ābelē;	Do it in a linden, in an apple tree;
Kā liepiņas man uzaugt,	That I may grow up as a linden,
Kā ābeles noziedēt.	That I may bloom as an apple tree.

—Latvian folk song

Potatoes with Cheese

5 potatoes, peeled and diced
oil for frying
¾ cups grated cheddar cheese
2 eggs

1. Fry potatoes in oil.
2. Mix cheese and eggs.
3. After potatoes are cooked, add cheese and eggs to frying pan.
   Mix well and fry, covered, about 5 more minutes.

MAKES 4 TO 6 SERVINGS.

Baked Potatoes

....

This recipe can include any leftover you might have: ground meat, vegetables like tomatoes and mushrooms, ham, onions, or minced herring.

10 to 12 boiled or uncooked potatoes, peeled and thinly sliced
leftovers
salt
2 eggs
1 cup milk
sour cream (optional)
butter
½ cup grated cheese

1. Preheat oven to 375 degrees F. Spread a layer of sliced potatoes in a 9 × 13-inch or 8 × 8-inch baking pan, depending on amount of leftovers. Then add a layer of leftovers. Continue to alternate layers of leftovers with layers of potatoes until dish is full, ending with a final layer of potato slices. Sprinkle salt over potatoes.
2. Mix eggs and milk together and pour over the dish. (Or add a few dollops of sour cream as desired.) Dot with butter. Sprinkle with grated cheese.
3. Bake for about 45 minutes (longer if you use uncooked potatoes). Season as desired.

MAKES 6 TO 8 SERVINGS.

Boiled Potatoes

*No Latvian cookbook would be complete without boiled pota-
toes, a staple in the Latvian diet. In the old days boiled potatoes
were often served with a milk porridge made by mixing barley or
wheat flour in a pot of milk. More recently the recipe has been
jazzed up with fat or roasted pork, butter, sour milk, herring, sliced
onions, or chives. Another recipe calls for frying small pieces of
smoked pork and onion in a pan. Add flour and, just before
serving, milk until the soup is thick. This is the basic recipe.*

about 15 small new potatoes, boiled with salt
dill
chives

Peel potatoes and sprinkle with dill and chives. Serve immediately.

MAKES 4 TO 6 SERVINGS.

Breaded Roasted Potatoes

Rivmaize cepti kartupeli

2 eggs
1¾ cups toasted bread crumbs
6 potatoes, boiled and peeled
1½ cups chopped tomatoes (about 2 tomatoes)
about 3 tablespoons butter for frying
salt
pepper

1. Preheat oven to 375 degrees F. Mix eggs and bread crumbs together.
2. Roll each whole potato in egg mixture. Bake until brown, about 45 minutes.
3. Lightly sauté chopped tomatoes in butter. Add salt and pepper to taste.

Top potatoes with chopped tomatoes and serve.

MAKES 6 SERVINGS.

Because much of Europe's Jugendstil architecture was destroyed during World War II, Rīga has perhaps the best Art Nouveau collection left in Europe. Architect Mikhail Eisenstein, who designed what is today the Stockholm School of Economics (above), designed some of his most famous buildings on Alberta and Elizabetes streets.

Potatoes and Tomato Sauce

3 or 4 strips smoked bacon, chopped fine
1 onion, chopped fine
4 or 5 potatoes, peeled and diced
parsley
pepper
½ cup tomato paste
1 tablespoon white flour
½ cup sour cream

1. Sauté bacon and onion together.
2. Add potatoes to bacon mixture. Add parsley and pepper to taste. Stir occasionally.
3. When potatoes are brown, add tomato paste. Mix well.
4. In separate frying pan, brown flour over low heat. Add to potato mixture and let simmer for about 5 minutes. Add ½ cup warm water if necessary. Add a dollop of sour cream before serving.

Serve as a side dish.

MAKES 3 TO 4 SERVINGS.

Layered Mashed Potatoes

5 or 6 potatoes, boiled and peeled
½ cup whole milk
1 onion, chopped fine
oil
¼ to ½ pound ground beef
salt
pepper
mushrooms (optional)
cooked carrots (optional)
2 eggs
3 tablespoons margarine
½ cup soft bread crumbs (about 2 slices bread)
¼ cup grated cheddar cheese
3 tablespoons butter
3 tablespoons grated cheddar cheese

1. Preheat oven to 375 degrees F. Mash boiled potatoes with milk.
2. Sauté onions in oil. Add meat and sauté until brown. Add salt and pepper to taste. Add mushrooms or cooked carrots to ground beef if desired.
3. Mix mashed potatoes with eggs. Add salt and pepper to taste.
4. Grease a 8 × 8-inch baking pan with margarine and line with bread crumbs. Spoon in half the potato mixture.
5. Cover the potato layer with ground meat. Cover with grated cheddar cheese. Follow with the rest of the potatoes.
6. Melt butter and pour on top. Sprinkle with cheddar cheese. Bake in oven until brown, about 30 minutes.

MAKES 6 TO 8 SERVINGS.

Bacon-Filled Potatoes

7 or 8 large new potatoes, baked
margarine
1 cup grated cheddar cheese
several strips of bacon, cooked and chopped fine
1 egg yolk
salt
pepper
sour cream

Preheat oven to 375 degrees F.

1. Cut the top off each potato and scoop out the insides. Set potato shell aside.
2. Mix the potato insides with margarine, ¾ cup of the grated cheese, the bacon, and the egg yolk. Add salt and pepper as desired.
3. Stuff the potato shells with the mixture. Sprinkle with the leftover grated cheese.
4. Bake until brown, 50 to 60 minutes.

Serve with sour cream.

MAKES 7 SERVINGS.

ANCIENT LATVIAN BELIEF: Lighting a cigarette from a candle will open the door to the world of ghosts and spirits. It is also said that if you do so, you will have no children.

Latvia's epic Lāčplēsis *by Andrējs Pumpurs (1841–1902) takes place 800 years ago in pagan Latvia. The epic recounts the exploits of a giant man who is part man, part bear, as is evident by his large, furry ears. He endeavors to protect his homeland through various battles. The government has recently revived the pre-war Order of Lāčplēsis, the nation's highest award for service in Latvia, which carries the motto "For Latvia."*

Although Pumpurs based his epic on existing Latvian folklore, the epic coincided with the growth of national consciousness in the 19th century. In the story Pumpurs represents the public's bitterness at the power Germans in particular wielded in Latvia after Christianizing German knights invaded Latvia in the 1200s.

The Bear Slayer
Rendition by Rita Laima Krievina
Edited by Michael Tarma

In the blue vault of the sky, in the castle of the God of Thunder, the Baltic gods gather to give audience to the Father of Fate. Here, in the place where eternal light resides, he tells them the story of Christ. He tells them that Christ's teachings have been accepted by nations of the world. But, the Father of Fate explains, people perverted those teachings to their own evil ends. And now these very people have decreed that the Christian faith will be brought to the lands of the Baltics.

The God of Thunder speaks up, warning those who have taken it upon themselves to carry the religion of Christ forth intend to occupy the Baltic region and make slaves of its people. He vows that he will do what he can to help the people of the Baltics defend themselves against those foreigners and their evil designs.

The gods and goddesses huddle amongst themselves and discuss how they can give assistance to the Baltic mortals. Staburadze, who lives in a crystal palace in the depths of the mighty

Daugava River, comes forward to tell the other deities of her encounter with a youth whom she saved from death. She would like to keep him with her beneath the river lest he return to the surface and turn into stone. The God of Thunder, however, proclaims that the youth has been blessed and that he is destined for glory.

The Slaying of the Bear

Some time later, the youth leaves the waters beneath the river. The chieftain Lieivarde adopts the youth as his own son. One day a vicious bear attacks the chieftain. The youth intervenes and wrestles the bear to the ground. Grabbing the beast by the jaws, he rips the bear apart with nothing but his hands. The old chieftain is amazed by the boy's strength and courage, and so he decides to reveal what has been said by the gods about the destiny of the impressive young man. He is to become a hero of his people. Henceforth, the youth is known as Lāčplēsis, the Bear Slayer. The chieftain provides him with a fine horse, a sword, shield, silver spurs, and a marten-fur hat. The Bear Slayer then rides off to gain wisdom in the ancient Burtnieku school of wisdom.

Descent into Hell

On his way to Burtnieku, the Bear Slayer asks for lodgings at the castle of Aizkraukle, which stands at a desolate spot, far from the shores of the Daugava River. It is a place of notorious gloom. Here the Bear Slayer encounters Spidala, the gorgeous but evil daughter of the chieftain of Aizkraukle. The Bear Slayer, in young manhood, is enraptured by the sultry, dark-eyed Spidala. But to his horror, he discovers that she has made a pact with the devil.

One night the Bear Slayer secretly follows Spidala into the Devil's Pit. He draws close to a large house. Inside, he witnesses evil that is ghastlier than he can imagine. He sees the decadent Spidala and other young witches undress and then cavort with wicked demons. They partake in a bloody feast of children's hands and squirming eels. The feast is then disrupted by the old Devil,

Crooked Cap himself. He explodes into the chamber on a golden carriage that is pulled by a fire-breathing dragon. The demonic bunch then encircle a trembling mortal. It is Kangars*, who is deemed by his people to be a holy man. But, as the Bear Slayer quickly discovers, Kangars is the most despicable and lowly of traitors. Kangars is spared from being chewed up by the Devil's dragon by promising to disavow his god and to betray his people. He condemns them to slavery at the hands of the foreigners now heading across the Baltic Sea.

The Bear Slayer has had enough of this hideous scene. He slips out of the house to make his way back to Aizkraukle castle. But an old witch sees the Bear Slayer and tells Spidala to dispose of him. She pursues him on a river, where the Bear Slayer's log is sucked down into the whirlpool of Staburags*—to what should be a certain death. But the gods spare him. The Bear Slayer wakes up unscathed in the crystal chambers of Staburadze, where he encounters the beautiful Laimdota, the daughter of the wise old chieftain Burtnieks. Her intelligence also matches her physical charms. It is love at first sight.

Eventually the Bear Slayer must take leave of the beautiful Laimdota. Back on the river, the Bear Slayer meets Koknesīs— another youth of legendary strength—and they become friends. Together, they journey back to the Aizkraukle castle, where the evil Spidala is shocked to find that the Bear Slayer is still alive.

After some time, the two friends, the Bear Slayer and Koknesīs, depart for Burtnieku castle to learn the wisdom of the ancients.

The Estonian Giant

Three soul-mates come together: the traitor Kangars, the hell-bent Spidala, and Dietrich, a German priest whose ship is saved on the stormy sea by the Latvian Livi tribe. Little do the Livi people know, they have actually saved their future oppressors from death.

Latvians often compare the traitor Kangars with Soviet-era turncoats.

Some years pass. The Bear Slayer and his friend Koknesīs continue their studies at Burnieku castle. They do not know that the traitor Kangars has given word to the Estonian giant Kalapuisis that this is a good time to pillage and plunder Latvian villages. Kangars and the evil Spidala are certain that the Bear Slayer will shrink from challenging the invincible Estonian giant, knowing he would meet his death.

As Kalapuisis goes on a rampage, the old chief Burtnieks summons warriors to face the Estonian tyrant. He promises his daughter Laimdota's hand in marriage to the man who defeats the mighty giant. The Bear Slayer, who is head over heels in love with Laimdota, leaps at the chance. He goes to face the Estonian giant and roundly defeats him. Later the two make peace. Kalapuisis says that the whole Baltic area is under threat and that they must unite their forces to defend their lands against the outsiders.

The Bear Slayer's forthcoming marriage to Laimdota is approved when he spends a night in the old Burtnieku castle. At the castle he defeats yet another ghoulish monster. An old castle and its storehouses of wisdom subsequently rise to the surface after lying for centuries under the lake's dusky waters. The young lovers immerse themselves in the ancient scriptures, which tell the secrets of creation.

Their bliss is cut short when Laimdota and the Bear Slayer's friend Koknesīs are kidnapped and then spirited away on a ship bound for Germany. The vessel is also carrying the Livi chieftain Kaupa to Germany and then on to Rome, where he is to learn more about the Christian faith. This is all a devilish scheme of the evil Spidala and the traitor Kangars, and it nearly crushes the spirit of the Bear Slayer. The villains lie to the Bear Slayer, telling him that Laimdota and his best friend have been lovers all along. Shattered, the Bear Slayer returns to his father's home, partly believing

---

The rock Staburags on the river Daugava is the site of a struggle between good and evil and represents national survival. The Daugava River is often portrayed as bearing the fate of the nation.

The epic hero Lāčplēšis on Rīga's Freedom Monument.

that the story is true. He then resolves to sail north to find the sublime daughter of Ziemelis. Perhaps this northern beauty will cool his feverish head and help him forget the sorrow that is raging in his heart.

The Great Deceit

Grand Rome, ancient Rome,
Where the Holy Father lived.
There he ordered the crusades
To conquer the land of St. Mary.
The Holy Father had deemed the Baltic to be St. Mary's land;
The sinning knights' sins were absolved by him.

In Rome, Christian missionaries plot the subjugation of the Baltic pagans. The Holy Father receives the priest Dietrich and the Livi chieftain Kaupa, who is enchanted with the riches laid out before him. He is also overwhelmed with doubt about his own gods. Kaupa promises to return home and to be christened together with his people. Back in his own country, hundreds of people toil, building the fortress of Rīga and its somber cathedral which spills so much misery into the surrounding lands. Priests and knights spread a wave of terror and oppression across the land.

The lovely Laimdota has been locked up in a cloister somewhere in Germany. She is rescued from the lusty advances of a German count by the Bear Slayer's friend Koknesīs. The two make their escape, boarding a ship bound for the north.

Meanwhile, the Bear Slayer has sailed even farther northward. At the edge of the sky, he encounters the legendary daughter of Ziemelis. Her eyes are like the color of the sky on a clear day in the north. The astonishing beauty is surrounded by her weapons of war, but she is kind and offers the Bear Slayer and his ship's crew a chance to rest. The exhausted wayfarers are led to a fabulous garden where they rest in the glow of a flame that shines up from the center of the earth. But the Bear Slayer becomes bored. He announces that it is time to pack up and return from whence they came. The lovely daughter of Ziemelis warns him that his trip will be full of dangers. He will have to take special care to avoid the Island of Dog Muzzles, which is full of blood-thirsty creatures.

But the Bear Slayer and his ship's crew do come across the Island of Dog Muzzles—where the hero barely survives an attack by vile beings. The weary crew finally makes it to the edge of the earth. One of the Bear Slayer's last heroic deeds before his final battle back home is to hack off the heads of three many-headed demons on the Last Enchanted Island, where he is miraculously reunited with Laimdota and his friend Koknesīs. It is here that he also manages to release a repentant Spidala from her pact with Satan, and afterwards she and Koknesīs become lovers.

The Bear Slayer's Demise

The Bear Slayer and Laimdota, and Koknesīs and Spidala are wed. The festivities, which take place on Midsummer Day, are overshadowed by a distant, fateful storm which is brewing misery for the Baltic people that will last for 700 years. One by one, the Livi and other tribes succumb to the German crusaders. In a last-ditch effort to defend their freedom, the Bear Slayer unites his people against the alien forces and succeeds in driving them all the way back to the walls of Rīga.

Victory, however, is short-lived, for the air is heavy with deceit.

A bitter and brooding Kangars, forsaken by his own kind, is sought out by the German priest Dietrich. The traitor Kangars then beseeches the Devil to learn the secret of the Bear Slayer's great strength. What is its source? What he learns is that the strength of the giant, the greatest hero of the land, is in his bearish ears!

Shortly thereafter, a band of roving knights come to the Bear Slayer's castle. A mysterious knight dressed in black steps forward and challenges the Bear Slayer to a fight. The Dark Knight knows about the source of the hero's strength, and in the course of the ensuing duel he duly lops off the Bear Slayer's ears, and infuriates the great giant. These forces of good and evil—the Bear Slayer and the Dark Knight—engage in an intense battle. Finally, as they swipe at each other and then wrestle to the ground, they both tumble over a cliff above the mighty Daugava River, and vanish underneath the dark waves forever.

Excerpted from the City Paper-The Baltic States, Parnu mnt. 67a, EE0001 Tallinn, Estonia.

Meat Dishes

Saule
Sun

The rhythm of life is most closely associated with the sun, which is said to possess healing properties. The sun symbol has been found on ornaments dating from the Early Iron Age. Because of its golden glimmer, amber, which first appeared in the Baltics around 2000 B.C., was often associated with the sun. Like the sun, it was thought to heal and was often worn as an amulet. Warriors wore axe-shaped amber pendants to protect themselves against being wounded in battle. The ax signified Perkons, who can fell even the mighty oak.

Tacitus wrote of the Baltic tribes: "They worship the mother of gods and images of the boar, signs of superstitious beliefs ... They are the only people to look for amber, which lies on the shore among the sea wrack. They sell it to their neighbors for a high price—which amazes and perplexes them."

Kālabad ik vakara　　Why each evening
Gaisa gali atsārkuši?　Are the edges of the air reddened?
Saule savus zīda svārkus　The Sun her silk skirts
Ik vakara vēdināja.　　Each evening airs.

—Latvian folk song

Jugendstil architecture.

Breaded Pork Chops

Karbonade

1 egg
3 tablespoons light cream
¾ cup dry bread crumbs
salt
pepper
6 pork chops
about ½ cup all-purpose flour
oil for frying

1. Beat egg with cream.
2. Mix bread crumbs with salt and pepper.
3. Tenderize chops with a small mallet. Dip chops in egg mixture
   and then flour. Coat with bread crumbs.
4. Fry chops in oil over high heat until brown. Reduce heat and
   cover for 4 to 5 minutes.

MAKES 6 SERVINGS.

Stuffed Cabbage

You can use any type of ground meat in this recipe. Pork is most popular. Beef or lamb is also good.

1 large head savoy cabbage
salt
1 small onion, chopped
1½ pounds ground meat
½ cup rice, cooked with pinch of salt
pepper
basil or hot sauce (optional)
1½ cups sour cream

1. Place whole cabbage in water and bring to a boil. Add salt.
2. When cabbage is slightly soft (9 to 12 minutes), set aside.
3. Sauté onion and ground meat. After the meat is mostly cooked, add cooked rice. Mix well and heat through.
4. Add salt and pepper to taste. If desired, add basil, more pepper, hot sauce to meat mixture. Set aside.
5. Carefully tear the whole leaves from the cabbage.
6. Make small meatballs from the meat mixture. Place one or two (depending on size, shape, and sturdiness) cabbage leaves on flat surface and place one meatball on leaf. Wrap the ball with the cabbage leaf carefully, folding all sides to cover filling.
7. Arrange the stuffed cabbage rolls snugly in a frying pan and fry over low heat for about 20 minutes. You should be able to fit 4 to 6 rolls in a frying pan at once.

8. Spread sour cream over cabbage rolls and cover. Let simmer for 45 minutes to an hour, turning the rolls carefully once or twice, until liquid collects at the bottom of the pan.

VARIATION: My friend Liga told me that she fries the rolls on both sides until brown before adding sour cream and 1 can (6 to 8 ounces) stewed tomatoes. She then covers the stuffed cabbage rolls and bakes them at 375 degrees F for 30 minutes to an hour, or until they are nicely browned.

MAKES 6 TO 8 SERVINGS.

According to ancient Baltic religion, it was prohibited to cut a tree, remove a dead branch, or kill an animal in a sacred grove. Nor was one allowed to cultivate the land around the sacred groves.

Sauerkraut and Sausage

3 cups sauerkraut
2 tablespoons oil
1½ cups chopped carrots (about 3 carrots)
1 pound smoked kielbasa, cut in bite-size pieces

1. Mix sauerkraut, oil, and carrots.
2. Add kielbasa and cook over medium heat, stirring occasionally, for about an hour.

MAKES 6 TO 8 SERVINGS.

Roast Pork Loin

·····························

2 pounds pork loin
salt
about 2 tablespoons flour
butter for browning
pork gravy (recipe follows)

1. Preheat oven to 450 degrees F. Sprinkle pork with salt to taste.
2. Roll in flour and brown in butter on all sides.
3. In a 9 × 12-inch baking dish, bake pork with the sauce from the frying pan and 3 tablespoons water until brown, 30 to 45 minutes. Then reduce heat to 250 degrees F to finish meat slowly, about 30 minutes. Baste occasionally with butter, adding water if necessary.

Serve with gravy.

MAKES 5 TO 6 SERVINGS.

Pork Gravy

When my friend Ieva made this recipe, she used milk straight from the cow. However, store-bought milk will do as well!

pork fat and bits
oil for frying
1½ cups chopped mushrooms
1 onion, chopped fine
2 tablespoons wheat flour
1 cup whole milk

1. Fry pork fat and bits in oil over medium to high heat.
2. Add mushrooms and onion and simmer 20 to 30 minutes.
3. Add wheat flour and the milk. Cook to desired thickness.

Serve with pork.

Noriet saule vakarāi
Koku galus veltīdama:
Liepai lika zelta kroni;
Ozolami sudrabiņa,
Sīkajam bērziņam
Dimantiņa lapiņām,
Mazajam kārkliņam
Uzmauc zelta gredzentiņu.

In the evening the setting sun
Bestows her gifts on the tops
of trees.
On the linden she rests a crown
of gold.
One of silver on the oak.
She gives the small birch
diamond leaves,
And on the osier she puts a
golden ring.

—Latvian folk song

Caraway Cutlets

....

1 pound chopped pork
1 pound chopped beef
3 pieces white bread, moistened
2 tablespoons caraway seeds
salt
pepper
2 eggs
juice from ½ lemon
3 garlic cloves, grated
2 onions, finely cut
2 tablespoons sour cream
1 tablespoon oil
2 tablespoons butter
2 cups green peas

1. Mix chopped pork and beef with moistened bread. Add caraway seeds. Mix well and let settle for 15 minutes.
2. Add salt, pepper, eggs, lemon juice, grated garlic, onions, sour cream, and oil.
3. Separate into large meatballs and flatten to form cutlets. Fry cutlets in hot frying pan in butter until brown. Reduce heat and cover for 4 to 5 minutes. After cutlets are cooked, add green peas to frying pan. Serve together.

MAKES 6 TO 8 SERVINGS.

Latvian Meat Balls

1 onion, chopped
3 tablespoons butter
2 tablespoons sour cream
salt
pepper
½ pound ground beef
1 tablespoon wheat flour (optional)

1. Sauté onion in butter.
2. Mix sour cream, 1 tablespoon water, salt, and pepper to taste. Add to frying pan and bring to a boil.
3. Add beef to frying pan. Separate the meat with a spoon and form small meatballs. Cook until browned. If necessary, thicken the sauce by adding the flour.

MAKES 3 TO 4 SERVINGS.

Pork with Young Potatoes

2 pounds pork, boned and cut into strips
pepper
2 eggs, beaten
2½ cups toasted bread crumbs
butter for frying

1. Pound strips of pork until very thin.
2. Cover both sides with pepper.
3. Dip pork strips into beaten eggs to coat.
4. Coat both sides of pork with bread crumbs.
5. Cover and fry in butter over high heat until brown. Reduce heat and cover for 4 to 5 minutes, turning occasionally, until brown.

Serve with boiled young potatoes.

MAKES 6 SERVINGS.

Pork Aspic

Cukas galas galerts

2 fresh pork hocks
½ pound lean pork (shoulder or tenderloin)
1 carrot, cut in small pieces
1 onion, cut in small pieces
1 bay leaf
1 clove garlic, crushed
3 peppercorns
½ cup chopped tomato
1 or 2 tablespoons gelatin
2 egg whites
salt
pepper
2 tablespoons chopped fresh parsley

1. Bring pork hocks and meat to a boil in plenty of water. Boil about 20 minutes.
2. Add carrot, onion, bay leaf, garlic, peppercorns, and chopped tomato. Simmer about 2 hours or until meat is tender. Remove from heat. Remove pork from broth and set aside.
3. Strain the broth in a sieve. Bring the strained broth to a boil again. Turn heat to low and let simmer.
4. Mix gelatin and water according to package instructions. Add to broth.
5. Beat egg whites. Add to broth. Season with salt and pepper to taste.

6. To serve, sprinkle parsley in the bottom of the serving bowls. Chop meat and place a few pieces in each bowl. Cover meat with broth.
7. Refrigerate for 24 hours before serving.

Garnish with parsley or mustard.

MAKES 6 TO 8 SERVINGS.

Liver
Aknu pastete

2 small onions, chopped fine
oil for frying
½ pound bacon fat
2 pounds liver, chopped
garlic
pepper
salt
7 tablespoons butter

1. Sauté onions in oil and bacon fat.
2. Add chopped liver to frying pan. Fry until cooked (6 to 8 minutes).
3. Grind liver mixture with onions, garlic, pepper, and salt in meat grinder or food processor.
4. Mix with butter. Refrigerate for 24 hours before serving.

MAKES 4 TO 6 SERVINGS.

Bobsledding is a favorite pastime in Latvia, and the bobsled track in Sigulda, built for the former Soviet bobsled team, is popular among bobsled enthusiasts. Part of the European luge championships are held here every January. We took a hair-raising, 70-second ride one summer day on the Mad Max, a wheeled bob constructed for summer months by the same Max who runs the track today. Rumor has it that Max celebrated his birthday by riding a shovel down the track's entire 1200 meters. Olga, another bobsled enthusiast who works at the track, has reputedly taken the ride on roller blades.

Sigulda is situated in one of the loveliest parts of Latvia among rolling hills, legendary caves, and medieval castles. Turaida Castle, built in 1214 by the Archbishop of Rīga, is one of its most famous. It was home to the legendary Turaida Rose, the burial site of a local beauty who died tragically in the 17th century. As legend has it, a young girl named Maija was sheltered in the castle after a battle. She grew into a great beauty. Although she had many suitors, her true love was Viktors, a gardener at the Sigulda Castle opposite. The sweethearts would meet at the Gutmanis Cave, halfway between the two castles. One day a desperate Polish suitor and his servant lured Maija to the cave. To persuade him to free her, she offered him the scarf from around her neck, which had been a gift from Viktors. She claimed that the scarf had magic powers that would protect her—even from his sharp sword. He took the challenge, swung at her with his sword, and killed her instantly. Unfortunately the Turaida townspeople accused Viktors of killing Maija and a date was set for his trial. On the first day of the trial, however, the Pole's servant appeared at the court and admitted his master's guilt. Viktors was freed and disappeared without a trace. The grave where he buried Maija at the Turaida Castle is still covered with roses today.

Turaida Castle.

Come Back Again
Nāc rūtā atkal

I sampled this recipe, a particular favorite of Latvians, in Sigulda. Its name invites guests to "come back again," as you can make this recipe from mostly leftovers.

THE BATTER:
4 eggs
10 tablespoons wheat flour
10 tablespoons oil
½ cup whole milk
½ cup water
pinch of salt
½ tablespoon sugar

THE FILLING:
1 onion, chopped fine
2 cups cooked meat, ground (see recipe page 64 to use
    leftover meat)
a few strips bacon or salted pork fat, cut in small pieces or ground
1 teaspoon butter
1 teaspoon prepared broth or water
salt
pepper
paprika
parsley
dill
chives

1. Mix batter ingredients together.
2. In another bowl, mix onion, cooked meat, and bacon together. Grind in meat grinder or food processor.
3. In frying pan, melt butter and add 1 teaspoon broth. Add meat mixture. Season with salt, pepper, paprika, parsley, dill, and chives to taste.

For final preparation:
2 tablespoons oil
toasted bread crumbs
butter

4. Heat oil in frying pan over medium heat. Fry pancakes in oil, using about 2 teaspoons of batter per pancake to make a paper-thin pancake or crepe.
5. Place a tablespoon of the meat mixture on the cooked side of the pancake. Remove from heat. Fold the edges of the pancake around the filling. Place on a platter strewn with bread crumbs. Right before serving, lightly sauté in butter until brown.

Serve with a salad, a cup of broth, sour cream, or applesauce.

MAKES 12 TO 15 SERVINGS.

Latvian Cutlets

Kotlettes

1 medium onion, chopped
¼ pound bacon, chopped fine
1 pound ground beef
½ pound ground pork
2 eggs
2 tablespoons sour cream
1 tablespoon milk
1 teaspoon cornstarch
salt
pepper
1 cup dry bread crumbs
oil for frying
parsley

1. Sauté onion with bacon until translucent.
2. In a large mixing bowl, mix beef, pork, eggs, sour cream, milk, and cornstarch together. The mixture should hold together well. Add more milk if it is too dry. Add salt and pepper to taste.
3. Roll mixture into small balls. Spread bread crumbs across a wooden board and roll the meatballs in the bread crumbs to coat. Flatten the balls slightly and make a crisscross pattern on both sides.
4. Heat oil in the bacon drippings in the frying pan. Fry meat patties over high heat until brown. Reduce heat and cover for 4 to 5 minutes.
5. Garnish with parsley.

Serve hot with boiled potatoes, diced carrots, and a green salad or dill pickles.

MAKES 8 TO 10 SERVINGS.

Fish Dishes

Zalktis
Serpent

The sign of Zalktis, or Serpent, which represents an ancient serpent cult, is often found on women's apparel and jewelry.

In Latvian mythology the harmless snake Zalktis was the guardian of wealth and well-being. Ancient Latvians often kept tame snakes in households and fed them with dishes of milk.

In this country you can often see snakes and various other creatures created by evil spirits flying in the sky at nighttime.

—From a 16th-century memoir of Latvia

Perch, roach, pike, bream, ruff, and carp are only a few of the estimated 25 species of fish that live in Latvia's lakes. The Baltic Sea, which has also been a major source of food and income for many generations of Latvian fishermen, offers sprats, eel, cod, salmon, sardines, and herring. Sprats (sardines) are especially popular tasty treats among the Latvians.

Seafaring provides some of the most interesting language studies of Latvian. Earliest loans in the Latvian language came from Livonian, a Finn-Ugric language native to Latvia of which 20 speakers still remain in Latvia. The Livonian word *laiva*, for example, survives as boat in Latvian as well. Latvian was also greatly influenced by the country's many foreign invaders. Old Russian, for example, gives loans in the areas of trade and religion: *cena* means price and *baznīca* means church. Middle Low Germans gave to the industries of craft, fashion, and agriculture: *ēvele* means tool, *kleita* dress, *torte* cake, *aptieka* pharmacy, and *bietes* beet. Although literary Latvian dates from the late 16th century and was developed by German pastors for peasant and domestic use, the 19th-century National Awakening saw Latvian finally as an official language. Words such as *vēsture* for history and *veikals* for store date from the 19th century. During Soviet times Latvian did not develop at all. For example, my friend Jānis, a technology expert in Rīga, pointed out to me that there are practically no Latvian technological words in existence. So far, Latvians must use Russian to talk tech.

Seasoned Sprats

2 tablespoons salt
1 tablespoon pepper
2 tablespoons sugar
2 pounds sprats (Baltic sardines)
2 lemons
dill

1. Mix salt, pepper, and sugar together.
2. Place a pinch of the mixture on a plate. Place a sprat belly up on the mixture. Repeat until the dish is full.
3. Cover dish and weigh it down. The fish is ready in 20 minutes. (Do not eat after 2 hours.)
4. Before serving, turn the plate upside down on another plate and lift carefully.

Garnish with lemon juice and/or dill.

MAKES 5 TO 6 SERVINGS.

Baked Trout

2 tablespoons melted butter
1 whole trout (substitute: pike or whitefish)
salt
pepper
dill
1 cucumber, sliced
1 onion, sliced
1 bay leaf
2 cups cream
chopped fresh parsley

1. Preheat oven to 375 degrees F. Spread melted butter on baking dish and place fish on butter. Sprinkle with salt, pepper, and dill.
2. Place cucumber and onion slices on and inside fish. Add bay leaf. Pour cream over fish.
3. Bake for 50 to 60 minutes.

Garnish with parsley before serving.

MAKES 4 TO 5 SERVINGS.

Herring Pâté

1 salted herring
1 onion, chopped
oil or butter for sautéing
2 potatoes, boiled
¼ cup sour cream
1 teaspoon vinegar
pepper
mustard
parsley

1. Soak herring in water overnight.
2. Clean herring and remove bones. Sauté onion in butter or oil.
3. Grind herring, onion, and potatoes together in food processor. Add sour cream and vinegar. Add pepper and mustard to taste. Mix well.
4. Place on a platter and shape as desired. Garnish with parsley. Serve with rye toast or crackers.

MAKES 4 TO 5 SERVINGS.

Various omens warned the ancient Latvians of impending bad fate. The worst signs were pigs and old women. Even today if a Latvian fisherman meets an old woman on his way to fish, he will often reconsider his fishing trip that day.

Herring Butter

1 or 2 herrings
1 large onion, chopped
butter for frying
1 large apple, peeled and chopped very fine
½ cup (1 stick) butter
¼ teaspoon nutmeg
2 tablespoons fine bread crumbs
3 tablespoons oil
pepper

1. Soak herring overnight in cold water. Remove skin and bones. Mince herring.
2. Sauté onion in butter. Mix chopped apple and sautéed onion with minced herring. Blend well in food processor.
3. Beat butter until light and fluffy. Add to herring mixture. Add nutmeg, bread crumbs, and oil. Add pepper to taste. Refrigerate until serving.

MAKES 4 TO 5 SERVINGS.

Poached Pike

1 pound pike (not fillet)
1 tablespoon finely chopped onion
parsley
salt
pepper
bay leaf
1 tablespoon sour cream
2 tablespoons chopped fresh cucumber
½ egg, hard-boiled and cut in small pieces
chives
dill
sugar
juice from 1 lemon

1. Clean the pike, setting aside the good pieces of fish. Boil the rest of the pike (the parts you don't want to eat) for about an hour for a nice fish broth.
2. Strain the fish broth in a sieve. Add the onion, parsley, salt, pepper, and bay leaf. Boil again.
3. Add the good pieces of fish. Let simmer until fish is cooked (about 45 minutes).
4. Remove fish pieces and set aside. Remove from heat and strain the broth.
5. Add sour cream, cucumber, and hard-boiled egg. Add chives, dill, and sugar to taste. Refrigerate.

To serve, place the pike pieces on a plate. Sprinkle with lemon juice. Cover with cold bouillon.

MAKES 2 TO 3 SERVINGS.

Fried Sprats

....

1 pound Baltic sprats or sardines
salt
1 tablespoon flour
butter for frying

1. Wash and clean fish. Sprinkle salt and flour on both sides.
2. Fry in butter.

Serve with boiled potatoes and melted butter.

MAKES 3 TO 4 SERVINGS.

Jugendstil architecture.

Tursad tulgu meie merde
Muda mingu muude mutsa

Let the cod come to our seas
Let mud go to the others' wood.

—*Livonian Easter song, from Kristi*
Salve's Fisherman's Work and the Sea
in the Livonian Folk Calendar

The Livi Coast, a strip of 14 villages along the Baltic Coast between Ģipka and Ovīši in the region of Kurzeme, is home to the last settlement of the ancient tribe of Livs, who arrived on Latvia's northern shores more than 5,000 years ago. This fiercely protected region seems lost in time. Elk bones are street signs. Ancient fishing boats lie on deserted beaches. Not a restaurant, hotel, or even a grocery store has opened shop in many of these towns. Liv residents rely on the shops-on-wheels that roll into town once a week. One local legend tells of a minister in the 16th century who turned into a werewolf at each full moon, a common problem in those days of rampant witchcraft. Even today, in order to keep his spirit from returning, residents solemnly keep his grave piled high with stones.

The Soviets were interested in decreasing the number of nationalities within the Soviet Union, and during the Soviet years the Livonians had to fight to keep their citizenship. Most gave up after long struggles with the KGB, but a few did succeed in keeping Livonian passports. Today 25 residents carry Liv passports and 20 speak the ancient Liv tongue.

Along the modern Livonian coast in the midst of traditional fishing villages like Košrags, Pitrags, and Vaide are fishermen huts, net huts, and smoke houses, as well as the August festival in Mazirbe when all Livs gather. Mazirbe is the largest town along the coastline and one of the only villages with in-town grocery shopping. Considered the spiritual capital of the region, it is home to the Livonian People's House, built in 1939. This Culture Center provides the history of the tribe and the area, as well as maps of the area. The Livonian flag of blue, white, and green symbolizing the sea, beach, and forest—all key elements of Livonan life—flies outside. In a lone phone booth nearby reads the inscription: "The installation of this pay phone (August 1996) is the first step in the telephonization of the Liv shore." The recently restored Mazirbe Church's cemetery includes the grave of a famous Livonian drunkard, to whom locals raise a toast after many rounds of beer.

It is written that the sea is the Livonians' field and the nets their plough. Both ancient and modern Livs were mostly fishermen, and many Liv houses still have a traditional *dumnamins,* a smoking house made of an old boat sawed in half. The Livs say that they can tell instantly whether fish has been smoked in the *dumnamins;* although it takes longer to prepare, it always tastes better. You're not likely to find a *dumnamins* handy at home, but you'll certainly find smoked sprat (or simply sardine) for this recipe in most stores.

Fried Sprats from Kurzeme

4 slices white bread
1 pound smoked Baltic sardines or sprats, cleaned and boned
pepper
salt
6 tablespoons butter
2 eggs
2 tablespoons sour cream

1. Preheat oven to 375 degrees F. Mix bread with 4 tablespoons
   water so that bread is mushy. Grind fish and bread in a meat
   grinder or food processor. Add pepper and salt to taste.
2. Melt butter and mix with eggs and sour cream. Add to fish mixture and mix well.
3. Bake in 8 × 8-inch baking pan for 30 to 40 minutes or until
   brown. Serve immediately.

MAKES 4 TO 5 SERVINGS.

Kurzeme Herring

1 pound salted herring
enough water or milk to soak herring
2 thick slices white bread
3 onions, chopped
½ cup (1 stick) butter
4 tablespoons sour cream
2 eggs
pepper
2 tablespoons dry bread crumbs
1 tablespoon grated white cheese

1. Preheat oven to 375 degrees F. Clean herring fillet. Soak herring in milk or water for a few minutes to soften. Cut in very small pieces.
2. Mix bread and ½ cup water. Press moisture from wet bread. Grind wet bread and fish together in meat grinder or food processor.
3. In a frying pan, sauté onions in butter. Add sour cream and turn heat to low.
4. Mix eggs and pepper. Add to frying pan. Mix well. Add fish mixture to frying pan. Mix well. Sauté 15 to 20 minutes.
5. Place the fish mixture in small ovenproof serving cups. Sprinkle with bread crumbs and grated cheese.
6. Bake for 20 to 25 minutes. Serve immediately. Good with rice.

MAKES 3 TO 4 SERVINGS.

Cod with Mushroom Sauce

1½ pounds cod
butter for browning
7 or 8 potatoes, boiled and cut in small pieces
6 cups bread crumbs (about a loaf)
1 tablespoon grated white cheese
1 teaspoon butter, melted

MUSHROOM SAUCE:
1 cup chopped mushrooms
butter for frying
4 tablespoons flour
½ cup sour cream
salt
pepper

1. Preheat oven to 375 degrees F. Brown cod on both sides in butter.
2. To make sauce, sauté mushrooms in butter. When soft, add flour, stirring constantly. When well mixed, add sour cream, and salt and pepper to taste.
3. Cover the bottom of a 8 × 8-inch baking pan with ⅓ of the mushroom sauce.
4. Next, place cod on sauce. Surround with boiled potatoes. Cover with the rest of sauce.
5. Sprinkle with bread crumbs, grated cheese, and melted butter. Bake for about 15 minutes.

MAKES 4 TO 5 SERVINGS.

Jugendstil architecture.

There are many sorcerers and witches in this country.
—German account of Latvia in the 16th century

~~~⊛~~~
Pike-Perch Canapés with Green Butter
••

Latvians still clean the perch in many traditional ways. One old Latvian fisherman who ice fishes near Rīga every winter recommends taking three crinkly bottle caps like those found on beer bottles. Nail the caps, edges out, to a piece of plywood. Dip the fish in boiling water for a few seconds and use your new tool to shuck the scales off.

1 pound pike fillet
salt
pepper
2 tablespoons wheat flour
1 egg, beaten
6 cups bread crumbs (about a loaf)
oil for frying
lemon slices

GREEN BUTTER:
3 tablespoons butter
dill
parsley
chives

1. Preheat oven to 375 degrees F. Cut fillet in 2 × 5- or 6-inch pieces. Sprinkle both sides with salt and pepper.
2. Sprinkle with flour. Pour beaten egg on both sides of canapés.
3. Sprinkle bread crumbs on both sides of each canapé.
4. Fry in oil over medium to high heat. When brown, bake for 5 to 7 minutes.
5. To make green butter, mix butter with dill, parsley, and chives well.

Serve fish with green butter, lemon slices, and roasted potatoes.

MAKES 3 TO 4 SERVINGS.

Cod Balls
············

Mencu Iodites

1 pound cod fillet, ground
½ cup potato flour
¼ cup heavy cream
1 teaspoon salt
ground nutmeg
3 onions, chopped fine

1. Mix ground cod, potato flour, cream, and salt in a bowl.
2. In a separate bowl, mix nutmeg and onions. Add to cod mixture.
   Grind mixture in food processor.
3. With a wet spoon, make cod balls. Boil in salted water for 6 to
   10 minutes.

Serve with boiled potatoes.

MAKES 2 TO 3 SERVINGS.

Herring with Mushrooms and Pickles

1½ pound salted herring
3 tablespoons oil
4 onions, chopped fine
1 to 1½ cups chopped sweet pickles (10 to 20 pickles)
1 cup chopped mushrooms (10 to 12 mushrooms)
1 tablespoon tomato paste
1 tablespoon dry bread crumbs
1 egg, hard-boiled and chopped

1. Preheat oven to 375 degrees F. Clean and dry fish.
2. Cut parchment paper in heart shape. Add oil to paper and place half the fish on the oil. Set the other half aside.
3. Sauté onions in a little oil. Add chopped pickles and mushrooms, stirring constantly.
4. Add tomato paste, bread crumbs, and hard-boiled egg to frying pan. Mix well.
5. Pour mixture over the herring on the parchment paper. Cover with the other half of the herring.
6. Wrap the paper around the herring. Bake for 30 to 40 minutes. Serve immediately.

MAKES 3 TO 4 SERVINGS.

ANCIENT LATVIAN BELIEF: If you don't remove your gloves before shaking hands, you'll shake your happiness away.

Salmon Roasted in Dough

1 pound salmon
salt
2 tablespoons oil
½ cup whole milk
2 eggs, separated
1 cup all-purpose flour
oil for frying
parsley
¼ cup (½ stick) butter, melted
juice from 2 lemons
lemon slices

1. Wash and clean salmon. Cut in pieces. Sprinkle a little salt on salmon pieces.
2. Mix oil, milk, and egg yolks with a pinch of salt. Mix well.
3. Beat the egg whites. After 30 minutes, fold the egg whites into milk mixture.
4. Dip salmon pieces in mixture. Coat with flour and set aside for about 30 minutes. Fry until cooked.

Garnish with parsley and serve with melted butter, lemon juice, and lemon slices. Serve with tomato paste with vegetables (recipe follows).

MAKES 3 TO 4 SERVINGS.

Tomato Paste with Vegetables

2½ tablespoons butter
¼ cup all-purpose flour
2¼ cups fish broth (see recipe page 78 or
    use prepared bouillon)
3 cups chopped carrots (about 6 carrots)
4½ cups chopped onions (about 6 onions)
1 can (6 ounces) tomato paste

1. Melt butter in frying pan. Add flour, mixing well. Add fish broth
   and mix well.
2. Add 1 cup chopped carrots and 1½ cups chopped onions and
   cook until soft.
3. Add tomato paste. Boil for 15 to 20 minutes. Strain soup, and
   bring to a boil again. Add the remaining 2 cups carrots and 3
   cups onions. Sauté until slightly crispy.

MAKES 3 TO 4 SERVINGS.

Brothers, we will go to Rīga,
In Rīga life is good.
In Rīga golden dogs bark,
And silver cocks crow.

—Latvian folk song

The Hanseatic city of Rīga, which turns 800 years old in 2001, is full of history, culture, and fairy tales, with castles, witches, and werewolves lurking at every cobblestone corner. We lived on the narrow, cobblestone street of Mucieneku (or Barrel maker's, named for the trade practiced here in ancient times) in Old Rīga near the 13th-century St. John's church. The church is best known for its small cruciform opening in the outer wall which is covered with a grating today. As legend has it, the church kept falling down, and the townspeople decided that it would stand only if someone were sacrificed. Two monks in the 15th century, hoping to be sainted, agreed to be sacrificed and immured themselves in a small niche in the church wall. They soon died. The Pope, who did not approve of their actions, did not saint them. The opening was filled in and forgotten until the spire of St. John's collapsed during a storm, and their remains were discovered. Out of respect for their memory, the cruciform was then opened again.

Enclosing oneself within the walls of churches was a popular custom in old Latvia, and the remains of others have been found during subsequent renovations as well. They weren't always martyrs, however. Another legend tells of a little girl who was enclosed in the Swedish gates, one of eight gates of Rīga's medieval defense wall, as punishment for trying to escape the plague.

Yet another Rīga legend involves the bell of 13th-century St. Jacob's Catholic Cathedral on the opposite side of Old Rīga. Called the "poor sinner's bell," it was bought in 1480 and erected outside the tower so that its sound would travel far. In the old days its ring called the townspeople to executions in the town hall square. Supposedly the bell also rang every time an unfaithful wife walked by. Its incessant ringing so irritated the women of Rīga that the bell was finally taken down. (The punishment for women committing adultery in those days was beheading—unless the adulterer was pardoned by the cheated husband and paid him 10 marks in silver and gave 3 marks in silver to the city.) The bell, evacuated to Russia for protection when Rīga was threatened during World War I, has never been found again.

The only Swedish gate of the original eight left intact. It was the gate through which the Swedish king Gustavus Adolphus entered the city in 1621.

Salmon Bread

Lasu maizites

about 4 ounces cream cheese with or without mushrooms
1 loaf fresh white bread, sliced
½ pound salmon
1 cup sour cream

1. Spread cream cheese on bread. Cover with salmon.
2. Spread sour cream over salmon.

MAKES 4 TO 6 SERVINGS.

Eel in Dill Sauce

½ pound eel
salt
1 teaspoon all-purpose flour
1 tablespoon butter
about 4 cups fish bouillon (see page 78 or
    use prepared broth)
¼ cup sour cream
1 egg yolk
2 tablespoons lemon juice
dill

1. Clean eel and cut into pieces about 1 inch thick. Sprinkle with salt and refrigerate for 1 hour.
2. In a frying pan, brown flour over low heat for about 5 minutes. When slightly brown, add butter, bouillon, and sour cream. Mix well.
3. Add eel to frying pan and fry 10 to 15 minutes.
4. Mix yolk and lemon juice together. Warm over low heat in separate pan. Add to sauce when heated.

Garnish with dill. Serve with boiled potatoes and sauce.

MAKES 3 TO 4 SERVINGS.

Carp in Beer

2 tablespoons wheat flour
½ cup (1 stick) butter
2 onions, chopped fine
¾ cup dark beer
5 tablespoons honey
pepper
salt
1 pound carp, cleaned
juice from 1 lemon

1. In frying pan, brown flour. When slightly brown, add butter and onions.
2. Add beer and bring to a boil.
3. Stir in honey. Add pepper and salt to taste.
4. Add carp and cover. Let simmer 10 to 15 minutes.

Garnish with lemon juice.

MAKES 4 TO 5 SERVINGS.

The Freedom Monument

No book about Latvia would be complete without a mention of the Freedom Monument, which stands at the entrance to Rīga's old town at the beginning of Freedom Street, *Brivibas iela* (formerly Hitlerstrasse and the Leņiņa iela), where the equestrian statue of Russian Tsar Peter I, conqueror of Rīga, once stood. Designed by Karlis Zale and Teodors Zalkalns and built through donations from the Latvian people, it was dedicated *Tevzemei un Brivibai* (To the Fatherland and Freedom) on the 17th anniversary of Latvia's Independence Day, November 18, 1935.

During pre-Soviet times two guards stood at the monument and well wishers placed flowers at its base. After the Soviets arrived, however, it was not permitted even to approach the monument. Indeed, one Latvian told me that the monument was jokingly referred to as a freelance travel agency. Anyone who dared place flowers at its base was immediately arrested and given a free one-way ticket to Siberia. Strangely enough, the Soviets never removed the monument, either because they believed that the three stars atop the monument (representing the three cultural and historical territories of ancient Latvia: Letgale, Zemgale, and Kurzeme) could pass for a reference to communism or for fear of the wrath of the Latvian people. They did erect a statue of Lenin to face it, however, which was removed in 1991. The Freedom Monument was also the site of an illegal rally on June 14, 1987, when 5,000 people gathered to commemorate the victims of Stalin's deportations.

Today, as in pre-Soviet times, two honor guards stand at the statue, whose base is cloaked with flowers. On anniversaries such as March 10, when thousands of Latvians were deported to Siberia, flowers extend from the monument as far into the old town as Philharmonic Square.

A series of sculpture groups circling the base depicts scenes from Latvian history and mythology and represents the many generations of Latvians singing, working, and fighting in the nation's long historic struggle for independence. "The Chain Breakers," a series of figures draped in chains, represents national liberation from foreign occupation. On another corner the ancient bard Vaidelotis tells of glories of ancient times. The legendary Bearslayer, a symbol of the heroic spirit of the nation, fights a bear in another scene. (See photo, page 115.) The National Liberation Army is represented at the Daugava bridgehead during the German attack on Rīga in 1919. Out of these figures rises a pillar topped by a bronze figure symbolizing Liberty.

Baked Salt Herring

8 halves salt herring
4 stale bread rolls
1 tablespoon butter
2 eggs, separated
2 tablespoons sour cream
pepper

1. Preheat oven to 375 degrees F. If necessary, soften the herring by soaking it in water.
2. Soak bread rolls in water. Press the moisture from them so that they are soggy but not dripping wet.
3. Grind herring and soggy bread together in food processor.
4. Mix butter, egg yolks, and sour cream. Add pepper to taste. Mix with herring paste.
5. Beat the egg whites. Add to paste.
6. Spoon a few tablespoons of mixture into several greased cup-cake pans or a small baking dish to about half full. Top with a few slivers butter. Bake for 30 to 40 minutes or until slightly browned.

Serve with potatoes and a green salad.

MAKES 8 SERVINGS.

Herring in Sour Cream

8 herrings
2 cups sour cream
2 tablespoons oil
½ cup white wine vinegar
6 bay leaves
10 peppercorns
3 medium onions, sliced
½ lemon, thinly sliced

1. Clean and soak herring in cold water for a night or two. Remove skin and bones.
2. Cut herring into 1-inch pieces. In a bowl, mix sour cream with oil and vinegar, beating thoroughly. Stir in bay leaves and peppercorns.
3. Pour enough sour cream mixture into a jar to cover the bottom. Alternate layers of herring pieces, sliced onion, and sliced lemon, following each layer with the sour cream mixture. Cover tightly.
4. Refrigerate overnight before serving.

MAKES 8 TO 10 SERVINGS.

Desserts

Moon

The moon, the symbol of warriors, is usually engraved on bracelets, swords, and other objects carried by warriors.

Es atradu uz celiņa
Dieva jātu kumeliņu:
Caur segliem saule lēca
Caur iemauktu mēnestiņš,
Pavadiņas galiņā
Auseklītis ritināja.

I found on the path
A steed Dieva had ridden.
Through the saddle the sun rose,
Through the bridle—the moon.
At the end of the rein
Rolled the morning star.

—Latvian folk song

Brandy Pudding
Rupjmaizes Kartojums

1 loaf scalded pan bread, or a dark bread made from parboiled
   flour, without crusts (or see rye bread recipe, page 39)
4 tablespoons oil
1 to 2 cups brandy (Bonaparte Brendijs is the
   Latvian brandy we use.)
2 cups heavy cream
5 tablespoons sugar
1 cup raspberry jam

1. Crumble bread into pot. Mix with oil over medium to high heat. Continue to stir so that the oil coats the bread crumbs. Add more oil if necessary.
2. After about 10 minutes, turn heat down low. Add about ½ cup brandy and stir. Cover and set aside for about 3 minutes.
3. Stir. Cover for about 5 minutes. Mix in ¼ cup brandy. Cover. After a few minutes, mix in another ¼ cup brandy. Stir well. The crumbs should be increasingly mushy. Continue to stir, adding brandy every few minutes until the crumbs are well-coated with brandy, and you've used all the brandy.
4. Cover and set aside for about 2 hours to allow the brandy to soak thoroughly into the bread crumbs.
5. In a separate bowl, whip cream and sugar together.
6. To serve, spoon about a ½-inch layer of bread crumbs in each serving bowl or cup. Follow with a layer of jam. Cover with whipped cream. Add another layer of bread crumb mix. Top with cream. Refrigerate before serving.

MAKES 4 SERVINGS.

Visapkārt ievu ziedi,	Bird-cherry blossoms all around,
Vidū balta ābelīte;	In the middle a white apple tree;
Visapkārt meitas dzied,	Daughters are singing all around,
Vidū meitu māmulīte.	In the middle the daughters' mother.

—Latvian folk song

Sculpture in Bastion Hill park.

Cinnamon Apples

4 apples, peeled and halved
6 tablespoons sugar
cinnamon
2 cups vanilla-flavored milk

1. Preheat oven to 350 degrees F, or you may use a microwave. Scoop seeds out of halved apples to form a hollowed-out middle. Place apples face up on a dish. Pour a little less than a tablespoon of sugar in the hollowed-out middle of each halved apple.
2. Sprinkle cinnamon over sugar and the face of the apple. Bake for about 30 minutes, or microwave for 3 to 4 minutes.
3. Serve vanilla-flavored milk on the side or pour it over baked apples.

MAKES 8 SERVINGS.

Drumstaly Pie

DOUGH:
1 (¼-ounce) package dry yeast
1 cup warm whole milk
3 cups all-purpose flour
2 tablespoons sour cream
½ cup (1 stick) butter
½ cup sugar
4 grains cardamom

SWEET BREAD CRUMBS:
14 tablespoons (1¾ sticks) butter
1 cup sugar
1½ cups all-purpose flour
peel from 1 lemon, ground
1 cup dry bread crumbs (optional)
3 eggs (2 are optional)

1. Dissolve yeast in warm milk by letting it stand for 5 minutes. Mix with the rest of the ingredients for dough and stir well. Place dough on greased 8 × 8 x ½-inch cookie sheet. Cover with oiled plastic wrap or a damp, clean dish towel and and set aside in a draft-free, warm room to rise for 1 to 2 hours.
2. In a mixing bowl, mix softened butter, sugar, flour, and ground lemon peel. Mix well. If desired, mix 1 cup bread crumbs with 2 eggs and add to sweet bread crumb mixture.
3. When dough has risen, brush with beaten egg. Sprinkle with bread crumb mixture. Bake until brown and crusty, about 30 to 40 minutes.

MAKES 10 TO 20 SERVINGS.

Apple Pie

DOUGH:
1 (¼-ounce) package dry yeast
3 cups all-purpose flour
1 cup warm whole milk
2 tablespoons sour cream
½ cup olive oil
¼ cup sugar
½ teaspoon salt

PIE FILLING:
about 10 apples, peeled and sliced
about ½ cup (1 stick) butter, melted
¼ cup sugar
1 teaspoon vanilla
1 tablespoon cinnamon
½ cup whipped cream
2 tablespoons confectioners' sugar

1. Dissolve yeast in warm water by letting it stand for 5 minutes. Add the rest of the ingredients for dough. Spread dough on a greased 9 × 12 × ½-inch cookie sheet. Cover with a clean, damp dish towel and set aside in a warm, draft-free place for 1 to 2 hours to rise.
2. Preheat oven to 350 degrees F. Cover with sliced apples. Pour the melted butter over the apples. Mix sugar, vanilla, and cinnamon and spread over apples. Bake until slightly brown.
3. Garnish with whipped cream and confectioners' sugar.

MAKES 15 TO 25 SERVINGS.

Although Latvian desserts are simple affairs made from fresh, natural products, the Latvians are also famous for their extremely sweet pastries, served throughout the country's cafés and for special occasions. Although not particularly practical for family events, these bite-sized morsels are tasty treats. While in Rīga, be sure to stop into Jaustrais Maiznieks, Brivibas 95, to sample the café's delicious pastries. Laima, Miera 22, and Staburadze, Valdemara 67, are also well-known sweets shops.

My friend Anita Plesūma, who is one of the directors at the Rīga Trade and Food Production School, graciously welcomed me to a few of its pastry classes, where I stood in white apron and cap with the other students and learned how to make the Latvian pastries served in cafés throughout the country. The school is little changed since it was founded, save an increase in the number of students, who do not pay to attend. My fellow students will go on to take positions as pastry chefs in many of the finest restaurants and cafés in Rīga.

The most popular sweet pastry is made from the following recipe.

Shortcake Pastry
....

Smilšu Mīkla

1½ eggs
14 tablespoons (1¾ sticks) butter
½ cup confectioners' sugar
1¾ cups all-purpose flour
dash of baking powder

1. Mix all the ingredients well. Place dough in a very thin layer in small cookie tins or an 8 × 8-inch cake pan, according to preferred shape.
2. Bake until brown (generally around 425 degrees F for about 20 minutes, depending on size).

Best when served with cream the following day.

MAKES 10 TO 12 PASTRIES.

Latvians sandwich or top the pastry with a variety of creams. Following are several popular Latvian fillings:

ᴬ᷎ᴼᴼᴯᴬ
Boiled Cream
••••••••••••••••••••••
Varitais krēms

You may want to decorate this and other pastries with tiny candies. To make them, mix lemon sugar with hot water and add a food coloring of choice. Refrigerate for a Jell-O-like consistency. Cut desired shapes and place them atop the pastries.

1 cup milk
½ cup sugar
2 eggs
1 cup flour
¼ cup (½ stick) butter
1 teaspoon vanilla sugar

1. Mix the milk and ¼ cup of the sugar in a pot. Boil slowly. Remove from heat.
2. In a bowl, mix eggs, the remaining ¼ cup sugar, and the flour. Add this mixture very slowly to the heated milk-and-sugar mixture while stirring. Continue to mix well.
3. Place the mixture over boiling water to steam. Stir constantly about 20 minutes or until mixture has thinned. Once it has reached the desired consistency, remove from steam and cool by placing pot in bowl of cold water.
4. In a separate bowl, whip butter until almost white and add vanilla sugar. Add milk mixture. Mix well for pudding-like consistency.

MAKES ENOUGH FILLING FOR 10 TO 12 PASTRIES.

Yogurt Cream
Yogurt krēms

1¾ cups yogurt
1 cup heavy cream
½ cup sugar
2½ cups juice from canned peaches or stewed peaches
1½ tablespoons gelatin

1. Mix yogurt, whipping cream, sugar, and peach juice together.
2. Make the gelatin according to package directions and add slowly to mixture while stirring.

MAKES ENOUGH FILLING FOR 10 TO 12 PASTRIES.

Cottage Cheese Cream
(Anita's favorite)

1 cup cottage cheese
½ cup flour
½ cup sugar
½ cup (1 stick) butter
2 eggs
1 teaspoon vanilla sugar

Strain cottage cheese. Whip all ingredients together for a light pastry filling.

MAKES ENOUGH FILLING FOR 10 TO 12 PASTRIES.

Rigās Melnais Balzāms

Rīga Black Balsams (*Rigās Melnais Balzāms*) is a favorite local beverage that often accompanies sweet pastries. Invented by local druggist Abraham Kunze, it has been produced in Latvia—and nowhere else—since 1755. The recipe for the thick, dark liqueur is a closely guarded secret, but Peruvian balsam oil, arnica blossoms, raspberry juice, orange peel, oak bark, and wormwood are listed among its ingredients. It is bottled in ceramic bottles similar to the sunproof clay pots used to store it centuries ago.

According to Latvia's pensioners, Black Balsams has great medicinal value. Its creator claimed, "It is advisable for different conditions: fever, stomach ache, toothache, headache, burns, chilblain, dislocations of limbs, white and red erysipelas, tumor, poisonous stings, fractured bones, and especially in cases of closed, stabbed, and chopped wounds." Catherine the Great, who was administered a dose when she fell ill during a trip to Rīga in the 18th century, instantly recovered—and never returned to Rīga.

You can buy Black Balsams in any local liquor store in Rīga. Serve as an aperitif or with coffee, Coca Cola, a shot of vodka, or over ice cream. Especially recommended is coffee with 2 tablespoons black balsam and 1 teaspoon brown sugar, topped with whipped cream and sprinkled with nutmeg.

Heavenly Manna
....
Debes manna

2 cups cherry fruit juice, cranberries, or red currants
1 tablespoon granulated sugar
3 tablespoons manna croup or Cream of Wheat
vanilla sauce (below)

1. Boil juice, sugar, and 2 cups water. If you're using cranberries or currants, cook until the berries are very soft and then strain through a sieve. Remove skins and bring to a boil again with about ¼ cup additional water. Strain again to remove skins.
2. Add manna croup and continue to boil until manna croup is soft. It should have the consistency of a thick porridge.
3. Pour into another bowl and let cool slightly. Stir frequently so that a skin doesn't form.
4. When the mixture is still slightly warm, whip with a mixer until it hardens slightly and is frothy. (In the old days, the man of the house used a wooden spoon to mix the *debes manna* and it took hours to harden.) Spoon into serving bowls and serve cold.

Serve with vanilla sauce.

MAKES 3 TO 4 SERVINGS.

Vanilla Sauce

2 cups whole milk
pinch of salt
1 stick vanilla
1 teaspoon cornstarch
1 to 2 egg yolks
4 heaping teaspoons sugar
1 egg white (optional)

1. Bring milk, salt, and vanilla to a boil.
2. Mix cornstarch with a little water. Add to milk. Bring to boil again. Set aside.
3. Beat the egg yolks and sugar until they become light and creamy. Add to milk and remove from heat. The sauce should be rather thick. If it's not thick enough, beat an egg white and add while hot. Refrigerate.

MAKES 3 TO 4 SERVINGS.

The life-giving forces of the sun, which is celebrated more fully in Latvia than in most countries, are recognized throughout the year in festivals and ritualistic customs. Just about every annual festival is traced somehow to the sun.

It's obvious, then, that springtime is the most important time of the year for chilly Latvia. The first day the Latvian farmer puts his cows out to pasture and lets the horses out of the barn, for example, is celebrated with a special drink of 87 secret ingredients concocted to ensure the good health and well-being of the farm-yard animals. Toasting these animals on the first day of spring shows that masters are taking care of their "smaller brothers." To keep in the spirit of things, make the noise of the animal that you wish well before you drink, a tradition in many families. After you toast, you eat a meal of bread rolls made from the recipe below or filled with the creamed cottage cheese, caraway seeds, radishes, or hemp butter. (Hemp was once grown throughout Latvia for hemp butter and other dishes; today, of course, it is illegal.) It's kefir to drink and tea tops off the meal.

Stuffed Rolls

6 soft raisin rolls
butter
¼ cup (½ stick) butter
crushed almonds
about ½ cup milk or cream
2 tablespoons rosewater
vanilla sugar
dried lemon peel
raisins
cinnamon
2 yolks, beaten

1. Preheat oven to 400 degrees F. Cut the top of each roll and scoop out the insides into a bowl. Spread butter lightly over the tops of the rolls and sprinkle with almonds.
2. Mix the bread removed from the rolls with milk or cream for the consistency of a porridge. Add the rosewater, vanilla sugar, lemon peel, raisins, cinnamon, and egg yolks.
3. Stuff the bread roll shells with the mix. Cover with the roll tops. Bake until slightly brown. (If you run out of stuffing, fill the rest of the rolls with whipped cream.)

MAKES 6 SERVINGS.

Fruit Jelly

You can use whatever kind of fruit you like: strawberries, raspberries, cherries, or blueberries.

juice of 1 lemon
½ to 1 pound fruit
3 tablespoons cornstarch
1 tablespoon sugar

1. Bring the lemon juice and ½ cup water to a boil.
2. Add the fruit and let it cook through.
3. Mix the cornstarch with a small amount of water and add to fruit sauce, stirring constantly. The longer you cook the liquid, the more syrupy and thicker it will become.
4. Pour liquid into a shallow dish. Sprinkle with sugar so that a skin doesn't form on top. Refrigerate.

Serve with milk, vanilla sauce (see recipe page 186), or whipped cream.

MAKES 5 TO 6 SERVINGS.

Jugendstil architecture.

The ancient traditions of Latvia centered not only upon the seasons and the sun, but also on significant family occasions. Family-oriented traditions generally relate to the important events in the cycle of life: birth, the naming of the child, marriage, and death. Choosing a child's name is of particular importance to Latvians. Names often reflect the bond between nature and people, as well as the importance of positive character traits. Latvians I knew had surnames like Kalns (hill), Lācis (bear), Vanags (hawk), and Bērz (birch tree). Jautriite (cheerful), Modriite (alert), and Gaisma (light) are all popular names for women.

If it is your name day, you are expected to host a party and be prepared for guests, who presumably have seen that it is your name day on the calendar, and well-stocked in food and drink at any time during the day. If you work in an office, you supply the food and drinks for a party there. Birthdays are a better deal. Friends then buy you dinner and drinks and bring flowers.

Look on any Latvian calendar, and you will notice one or more names written on nearly every day of the week. The names indicate the day dedicated to that particular name or names. Until recently, Latvians usually named a child one of a few traditional names, and relatively few names appeared on the Latvian calendar. Today, however, more and more new names are being introduced to Latvia, and, in turn, more names are appearing on Latvian calendars. To introduce a new name day is no small feat. In order for a new name to appear on the calendar, it must be introduced by application to the Name Day Committee in Rīga. Its members decide whether or not to accept the new name in the calendar. More than 200 new names were proposed this year alone—and an estimated 870 women's names and 700 men's names are already included on each yearly calendar. Still, some foreign names have even managed to secure a day for themselves in recent years. Turn to October 29 and you'll see the name Elvis!

Although simple pastries are the most popular food served on name days, any of these desserts will do for such a celebration.

Sweet-Dough Pastries

DOUGH:

¼ cup water
salt
1 egg
1 cup all-purpose flour plus extra for kneading
1 teaspoon lemon juice
butter, softened

1. Mix all ingredients except butter and set aside for about 15 minutes. Roll out and set aside another 15 minutes. Roll out dough again using plenty of flour.
2. Shape dough into a large rectangle, 12 × 6 × ½ inch thick. Dot with softened butter that is at the same temperature as the dough.
3. Fold about two thirds of the dough over evenly. From the opposite end, fold the remaining third over to meet the first folded two thirds.
4. Fold the same side again, halfway over. Set aside for about half an hour. Place in refrigerator to cool so that the dough will rise well when it's baked. It should take about 15 minutes.

FILLINGS:

Apple and Cinnamon Pastry

2 or 3 cups peeled, thinly sliced apples
½ cup sugar
4 tablespoons cinnamon
1 egg

1. Take dough out of the refrigerator. Roll gently out. Cut in half and put half back in refrigerator.
2. Roll out the remaining half in plenty of flour, until about ½ inch thick. Sprinkle a 9 × 9-inch baking pan with water and fit the dough snugly into pan so that the edges of the dough rise up around the pan edges. Poke fork around the dough and put back in refrigerator for about 15 minutes. Preheat oven to 425 degrees F.
3. Bake for about 15 minutes or until slightly brown. Cover completely with sliced apples.
4. Mix sugar and cinnamon. Cover apples completely with sugar and cinnamon. Take unbaked pastry out of refrigerator and cover the apples with it so that the apples do not show.
5. Beat the egg well. Brush the top of the pastry with beaten egg.
6. Bake for 15 to 20 minutes or until brown.

MAKES 6 TO 8 SERVINGS.

Cheese Pastry

1 egg
butter
1 cup grated mild white cheese
mint leaves

1. Preheat oven to 450 degrees F. Take dough out of refrigerator and roll out, using plenty of flour, to about ½ inch thick. Cut small, round pancakes (about 2 inches in diameter) using can or cookie cutter.
2. Beat egg. In half the pancakes, cut small round holes in the center of each pancake to form a ring. Reserve cut-out centers for later. Brush egg over ring. Take one of the uncut pancakes and place one of the pancake rings carefully on top to form the first layer in a stack. Place another ring on top of first ring. Between each level, brush the beaten egg. Do the same with the remaining pancakes, making each into a 3-level stack. Use the cut-out center to make more rings when necessary.
3. Bake for 10 to 15 minutes.
4. Whip butter and cheese together. Fill pastries with cheese mixture. Garnish each with a mint leaf.

MAKES 6 TO 8 SERVINGS.

Ear Pastry

sugar
nuts (optional)

1. Preheat oven to 425 degrees F. Take dough out of refrigerator. Roll out to about ½ inch thick. Take one end and carefully roll it until you reach the middle. Roll the other end to the middle to meet it.
2. When two sides meet, roll one on top of other and press together firmly. Cut pieces about 1 inch thick. The pastry should look rather like an ear. Cover with sugar. Place flat on pan and bake for 5 to 7 minutes. If you prefer a pastry with nuts, roll the pastry as above and cut very thin pieces. Cover with preferred nuts, pressing some of the nuts into pastry. Bake.

MAKES 8 TO 10 SERVINGS.

Caraway Strips

about ½ cup caraway seeds
salt

1. Preheat oven to 425 degrees F. Take dough from refrigerator. Roll out to ½ inch thick. Cover completely with caraway seeds and some salt.
2. Slice 4 × 3-inch strips from dough. Cut each strip into about three pieces, so that each piece is about 4 × 1-inch. Twist each strip around twice. Sprinkle pan with water. Place twisted strips in pan and bake for 5 to 7 minutes. This snack is especially good with beer.

MAKES ABOUT 20 STRIPS.

Sweet Apples

dough (see recipe page 191)
10 whole small apples, peeled
½ cup granulated sugar
½ cup cinnamon
confectioners' sugar

1. Preheat oven to 400 degrees F. Cut dough in squares large enough to be able to wrap an apple.
2. Bore hole in the middle of each apple to remove seeds and core.
3. Mix equal amounts of granulated sugar and cinnamon and pour mixture into hole in apple.
4. Wrap dough around apple, dumpling-style, so that opposite corners meet. Bake about 15 minutes.
5. Cover with confectioners' sugar before serving.

MAKES 10 SERVINGS.

ANCIENT LATVIAN BELIEF: Taking a knife from the hand of another person will make you enemies.

Alexander Cake

This cake became enormously popular around the time that the Russian czar Alexander came to visit Rīga almost 200 years ago. Although there are many different recipes for the cake, this is my favorite.

3½ cups all-purpose wheat flour
1 cup granulated sugar
pinch of salt
dash of vanilla
1¾ to 2 cups (3½ to 4 sticks) butter, softened
1 cup red or black currant jelly (substitute: 1 cup raspberry jam)
2 cups confectioners' sugar
4 tablespoons lemon juice

1. Mix flour, sugar, salt, and vanilla together. Add butter and knead until dough holds together. Divide into three parts. Wrap in plastic, and refrigerate overnight.
2. The following day, roll out each part to a ½-inch thickness and allow dough to reach room temperature, 1 to 2 hours. Preheat oven to 300 degrees F and then lower heat to 250 degrees. Bake each layer about 10 minutes or until golden yellow.
3. Let the first layer cool a few minutes. Spread ½ cup of the jelly over layer. When second layer has baked, cover the first layer with the second and spread with the remaining ½ cup of the jelly on the pastry. Top with final layer.
4. Let sit overnight. Mix confectioners' sugar with lemon juice. Spread icing over cake in a thin layer.

MAKES 6 TO 8 SERVINGS.

Silā man rudzi sēti
Silā dēti ozoliņi;
Zied rudzīši, san bitītes
Pats prieciņa nevarēju.

In the pine woods my rye has
   been sown.
In the pine woods are my
   hollowed oak trees;
The rye blooms, the bees hum,
I am beside myself with joy.

—Latvian folk song

Layered Rye-Bread Dessert

Use whatever kind of jam or fruit compote you like. Apple,
plum, lingonberry, and cranberry are popular.

3 or 4 slices stale rye bread, grated (see rye bread recipe page 39)
1 tablespoon sugar
¼ to ½ cup whipped cream
¼ cup jam preserves or fruit compote
Lightly brown the rye bread and sugar in a frying pan.

1. Layer a bowl with whipped cream, rye bread, and finally jam.
   Repeat until the bowl is full.

MAKES 3 TO 4 SERVINGS.

The Tale of Sprīdītis
(abbreviated version)

The children's play by Anna Brigadere's (1861–1933) was popular not only among Latvian children but among adults as well. Many saw Latvia in the tiny, fearless Sprīdītis, who triumphs over enemies far greater and more numerous than he.

A tiny young man named Sprīdītis is sleeping in the forest one day when he is disturbed by a local lord. Annoyed, Sprīdītis threatens to kill the lord. The lord, amused by the tiny man's pluck, decides that he will marry Sprīdītis to his beautiful daughter if Sprīdītis can defeat a bear. Sprīdītis cunningly traps a bear in a barn, but when he goes to claim his bride, the lord tells him that he must kill 12 robbers before he can have her hand. Sprīdītis succeeds by tricking the robbers into killing each other. Still the lord is reluctant to give the hand of his daughter. Instead he tells Sprīdītis that he must drive the enemy out of the land before the two can marry. Sprīdītis mounts a horse and meets the enemy waving a sword and shouting, "Frog! Frog!" The enemy commander, who thinks that a god from heaven has come to punish him, flees. And Sprīdītis marries the lord's daughter.

Swimming Islands

Peldosas salas

7 egg whites, whipped
1 teaspoon salt
2 cups vanilla-flavored milk

1. Bring salted water to a boil. Carefully spoon 4 or 5 tablespoons of whipped egg white (or as many as will fit on the surface of the water) into the boiling water. Each spoonful should float on the surface separately. They will harden slightly.
2. After about 5 minutes, remove the egg whites from the water and refrigerate.
3. To serve, pour vanilla-flavored milk into serving cups. Place one of the "islands" in each serving cup.

MAKES 4 SERVINGS.

Custard

······
Bubbert

Serve this with a red fruit sauce. To make your own, mix straw-berries or raspberries and a small amount of sugar in a food processor.

2 cups whole milk
1 stick cinnamon, crumbled
salt
dried lemon peel, grated
4 tablespoons wheat flour
2 eggs, separated
3 tablespoons sugar

1. Boil 1¾ cup of the milk with cinnamon, salt, and dried lemon peel.
2. Mix wheat flour and the remaining ¼ cup milk for the consistency of a thick porridge. While stirring, gradually add to boiling milk. Boil about 1 minute.
3. Beat egg yolks and 2 tablespoons of the sugar until light and creamy. Add to hot milk. Boil 1 minute.
4. Remove from heat. Stiffly beat egg whites with the remaining 1 tablespoon sugar. Fold egg white mixture into the hot milk. Refrigerate.

MAKES 6 SERVINGS.

Jāņis Rozentāls (1866–1916), who is considered one of Latvia's most famous painters, lived and painted on the top floor of this Jugendstil building.

Dried Fruit and Bread Soup

3 small loaves dark bread, crumbled
½ cup (1 stick) butter
1 cup dried apples
1 cup dried apricots
1 cup raisins
1 tablespoon cinnamon
4 tablespoons sugar
1 cup heavy cream or whole milk

1. Bring 6 cups water to a boil.
2. In a frying pan, fry bread crumbs in butter, stirring occasionally, until well browned.
3. Add crumbs to boiling water and turn heat to low. Cover and let simmer about 20 minutes.
4. Add dried apples, dried apricots, and raisins. Mix well.
5. Add cinnamon and 2 tablespoons of the sugar. Refrigerate.
6. Whip heavy cream with the remaining 2 tablespoons sugar.

Serve with a dollop of whipped cream or cover with whole milk.

MAKES 8 TO 10 SERVINGS.

Baltic White Bread Pudding

Baltmaizes sacepums

3 slices white bread, without crust and crumbled
½ cup cold whole milk
4 eggs, separated
¼ cup (½ stick) butter
¼ cup sugar
1 cup dried apples

1. Preheat oven to 350 degrees F. Mix all but a few tablespoons of the bread crumbs with cold milk.
2. Mix the egg yolks, butter, sugar, and apples together. Add to bread crumbs. Mix well.
3. Stiffly beat the egg whites. Fold them slowly into milk mixture.
4. Grease a 9 × 9-inch casserole dish with butter and line with bread crumbs. Fill with bread pudding and bake for 25 minutes.

Serve warm or cold.

MAKES 4 TO 5 SERVINGS.

Legend has it that when the German missionaries arrived around 1200, they requested enough land in Latvia to cover with an oxhide. When the Latvians agreed, they cut an oxhide into thin strips and encircled the area of present-day Rīga. They claimed everything within it as their own.

Drinks

∃∣E

Usins
awakening

Usins, the patron of horses, was first known as the god of light. He is most often celebrated in springtime when the horses first see daylight after a dark winter in the barn. His sacrificial offering was a prize rooster.

Rīga street scene.

Schnapps

lemon peel from 1 lemon
1 tablespoon sugar
1 liter vodka

1. Add lemon peel and sugar to vodka. Let sit at least 5 hours or overnight, shaking up the bottle once in a while.
2. Filter if necessary and dilute with cold water.

MAKES 1 LITER BOTTLE.

Latvian Champagne

Just before the leaves appear on the birch trees in the spring (for it's too late after they've appeared), many Latvians head for the country to make champagne. They tap the birch tree and drill a hole to gather the juice from the tree. After the juice is collected, it is filtered. Add a few raisins, a lemon peel, a small black currant stick, and 2 teaspoons sugar to the juice, and seal the bottles with corks and sealing wax. After about three months—just in time for Jāņi (see page 226), the champagne is ready to drink. Add sugar as desired. You can also drink the ginger-ale juice when it is first tapped from the tree. Juice from one tree will fill about 100 liter bottles.

Sweet Rhubarb

10 stalks rhubarb, peeled and cut in small pieces
sugar
cinnamon
cloves
sugar or fruit syrup (about 2 cups water per 1 to ½ cups sugar)
sweet whipped cream

1. Boil rhubarb with sugar, cinnamon, and cloves for about an hour, or until the rhubarb is very soft. It will continue to soften as it cools. Refrigerate.
2. Add sweet syrup and mix well.
3. Serve with a dollop of whipped cream.

In the country, rhubarb is also eaten raw with granulated sugar as a snack.

MAKES 6 TO 8 SERVINGS.

Other Boiled Juices

Boiled juices, *kissles*, are very popular in Latvia especially in summer. Thickened with starch and prepared as a soup, they can be made from any fruit or berry that is strained through a sieve or diced very fine. First, mix 1 cup water and 1 cup sugar and boil until sugar has dissolved. Add the berries, watching so that they do not overcook. Slowly add 1 or 2 tablespoons potato- or cornstarch (mixed with a small amount of cold water), keeping an eye on the thickness of the sauce. Spoon off the foam during the boiling process. Once the berries are cooked, you can remove them and add more berries to the sugar syrup. Sprinkle sugar on top so that a skin doesn't form.

Let raspberries and strawberries sit in sugar overnight before boiling. Boil hard berries like cherries in a small amount of water until soft before boiling in sugar syrup. Red currants and other juicy berries should be strained through a sieve first and the skins discarded.

When a girl marries, the girl dies and a wife is born in her place.

—Latvian proverb

Although modern Latvian weddings are joyous events—and a good excuse for a long party—in ancient times they were considered tragic occasions. Marriages in those days usually meant that a daughter of the house was being sent to live among strangers.

Ai Laimiņ licējiņa,
Kā tu biji nolikuse:
Atstāt tēvu, māmuliņu
Iet pie sveša cilvēciņa.

Oh Laima, spinner of fates,
Why have you decreed
That I must leave my parents
For a stranger?

Most ancient bridal customs are practiced only in jest today. Wedding songs and games play out the traditional "abduction" of the bride, who has "protectors" to save her from abduction, the following flight from her pursuing kinsfolk and the paying of ransom for her dowry.

Other customs are also a strong part of the ceremony. After the marriage the couple breaks a plate; the number of broken pieces indicates how many children they will have. In addition, everyone brings flowers to the bride for good luck. Perhaps most important is the symbolic replacement of the girl's coronet (today's bridal veil) with a woman's scarf, to mark her transition from single to married life. *Mice,* the ancient word for marriage, literally meant "taking off the crown." Traditionally girls wore garlands until marriage, when the garland was exchanged for the traditional crown of her region. The Latgale crown is narrow and flexible; the Courland region's is generally a metal crown; Zemgale's is narrow and stiff. This new crown covers her forehead, which is considered a thing of great beauty and wisdom. Once covered, only the husband is allowed to see it. As part of the ritual, the mother-in-law places the new crown on the bride, who refuses it several times before finally accepting it.

Lai raudāja, kas raudāja,	Weeping, who's been weeping?
Meitu māte, tā raudāja:	The maiden's mother has wept.
Trūkst klētī, trūkst stallī,	The storeroom is empty,
Trūkst mātei miļas meitas.	the cow shed is empty,
	the mother misses her daughter.

—Latvian folk song

Holiday Foods

> Our masters write, the sun writes,
> Marking my good brothers;
> Men write in books;
> The sun, in the maple leaf.

—Latvian folk song

St. Anthony's Day

Although St. Anthony's Day (January 17) is not largely celebrated in Latvia now, it is one of the first festival dates on the ancient Livonian calendar. St. Anthony was the patron saint of domestic animals and especially of hogs. In the old days it was said that in order for the hogs to thrive, a hog's head must be cooked and eaten and the bones taken to the forest. Also, combing your hair on St. Anthony's Day would bring lice to the hog. Finally, working with wool or linen would bring punishment by the hogs, who would eat your lambs if you worked with wool and tear up your fishing nets if you worked with linen.

Pig Snout

Boil, salt, or smoke whole or half of the pig's head. Serve it with fresh green apples, stewed cabbage, or other roasted or stewed vegetables.

Shrove Tuesday

The netmaking fork should be out of the house by Shrove Tuesday.
—Ancient Latvian proverb

Shrove Tuesday was often considered the beginning of spring in ancient Latvia. For fishermen, especially along the Livonian coast, this was the date when all fishing nets and preparations were to be finished. If "the netmaking fork" wasn't out of the house by then, a fork was tied to the back of the fisherman who lived there. Shrove Tuesday was also a time for fishermen to meet over a plate of these pancakes and find a fishing partner for the upcoming season.

Buckwheat Pancakes

¼ cup warm water
1 (¼-ounce) package dry yeast
1¾ cups wheat flour
1¾ cups buckwheat flour
teaspoons salt
1¼ cups boiling water (or more as needed)
eggs, separated
¼ cup (½ stick) butter

1. Dissolve the yeast in the warm water by letting it stand for 5 minutes. Add the wheat and buckwheat flour and salt. Knead the dough. Place in a clean bowl that has been lightly coated with oil and cover the bowl with oiled plastic wrap or a damp, clean dish towel. Let rise in a warm place for 1 to 2 hours.
2. After dough has risen, add boiling water until the batter flows easily from the spoon. Beat well with a wooden spoon for 10 to 15 minutes. (If the batter tastes bitter, add more wheat flour.)
3. Beat the egg yolks, and add to batter.
4. Beat the egg whites until stiff but not dry.
5. Melt butter over medium-high heat. Fold the egg whites into the batter just before pouring into frying pan. Use 1 to 2 tablespoons per pancake so that pancakes are ¼ to ½ inch thick.
6. Fry until a brown crust forms. Serve immediately.

Serve with melted butter and sour cream or salted herring mixed with sour cream (3 herrings per 1 cup sour cream). During celebrations vodka is also served alongside the pancakes.

MAKES 12 TO 15 SERVINGS.

Easter

Christianizing Latvia wasn't easy for the German missionaries who arrived around 1190. As soon as they left the countrymen on their own, the Latvians are reported to have "jumped into the river to wash off their baptism."

Easter, however, combines both Latvian's pagan traditions and its more recent Christian ones. It corresponds with *Lieldienas*, or "Big Day," which celebrates the arrival of the sun, as well as love, light, and fertility, to this northern land. After long winters the Latvians, eager for the long summer days, take this celebration seriously and joyfully welcome the sun with songs and dances. March 21 was traditionally considered the Big Day, and March 22 and 23 considered the second and third days of spring.

The swing, the symbol of the season, literally symbolizes the "swinging in" of spring. In each town one honored person is elected to choose a tree for the swing. Once elected, he or she has the job for rest of his life. Several beliefs center upon the swing. Swinging high toward the sun assures tall grains, a good harvest, and few mosquitoes. Disagreeable or unfriendly thoughts should not be entertained while swinging, although you'll protect yourself from them if you carry an egg, the symbol of fertility, while you swing. Eggs from black hens are especially powerful. Also, burying an egg under your neighbor's house drives away any unfriendly thoughts he may have toward you. Finally, you can protect yourself from evil throughout the year by burying an egg under the swing. You can visit the swing celebration at the open-air museum in Rīga during the week before Easter.

The swing also symbolizes fertility. If a man throws an egg over the swing and catches it on the other side, he'll soon find a wife. If he's married, he'll have a child within the year.

The person who rises first on *Lieldienas* wakes the others by hitting them with pussy willow branches, wishing "sickness out, health in!" They sing the following song:

Šūpo mani, māmuliņa
Vālodzītes šūpulī
Lai es loku valodiņu
Kā locīja vālodzīt.

Nokul mani, māmuliņa,
Ar vītola žagariņ
Lai es augu tik lokana
Cik vītola žagariņš

Rock me, mother,
In an oriole's cradle.
Then I will speak and sing
As nice as an oriole.

Thrash me, mother,
With a willow's switch.
Then I will grow up
As flexible as a willow birch.

In addition to swings and eggs, birds are also considered symbols of spring. Large birds symbolize dark forces that must be driven away, while small birds welcome springtime. They are also thought to be the souls of those who have gone on to the "World of the Other Sun," and spring is a time to pay tribute to them.

Nākat putnu dzinējiņi	*Šūvo! Šūvo!*
Pa kruminu kruminiem	*Šūvo! Šūvo!*
Nākat putnu dzinējiņi	*Šūvo! Šūvo!*
Pa sētmaļu sētmaļiem	*Šūvo! Šūvo!*

Aizjemate sīkus putnus	*Šūvo! Šūvo!*
Pa zariņu zariņiem	*Šūvo! Šūvo!*
Sīki putni šaizemē	*Šūvo! Šūvo!*
Vilki lāči Vāczemē	*Šūvo! Šūvo!*
Mēs putniņus nodzinuši	*Šūvo! Šūvo!*
Vilki, lāči Vāczemē	*Šūvo! Šūvo!*

Come in, drivers, from every bush,
from every yard! Drive in all small
birds to our land, drive away all
wolves and bears to farland!

Easter Eggs

Although this Easter egg recipe following sounds suspiciously like standard scrambled eggs, there's a ritual to making the dish. Traditionally each person pokes a hole in either end of an uncooked egg. He then blows gently into the hole until the egg pours out the opposite hole into a dish. (The shells are saved and later dyed.) After each person has contributed an egg and a pinch of spice (gathered the day before Summer Solstice, or *Jāņi*, the year before—see page 226), the eggs are cooked over a large open fire outdoors and eaten straight from the frying pan.

8 eggs
spices
a few teaspoons flour
about ¼ cup whole milk

1. Mix the eggs together in a bowl.
2. Add several pinches of preferred spices and flour.
3. Scramble with milk in frying pan.

Serve immediately.

MAKES 4 TO 6 SERVINGS.

Peasant-Style Scrambled Eggs
Olu kultenis zemnieku gaumē

This Easter egg dish is simply a variation on the recipe above.

eggs
salt

1. Preheat oven to 350 degrees F.
2. Whip eggs and salt together. Place mixture into greased fire-proof ceramic bowl and bake until brown, about 30 minutes.

Serve with natural rye bread and butter.

Easter Wreath
Lieldienu vainags

FOR DOUGH:
(¼-ounce) packages dry yeast
1½ cups all-purpose flour
1 teaspoon sugar
½ cup whole milk (room temperature)
salt
tablespoons margarine

FOR FILLING:
1 cup thinly cut almonds
½ cup sugar
tablespoons vanilla sugar
tablespoons currants
5 tablespoons condensed milk
tablespoons rum

FOR GLAZE:
¾ cup confectioners' sugar
splash lemon juice
small sugar eggs for decoration

1. Dissolve yeast in warm water by letting it stand for 5 minutes. Sift flour into a bowl and press indention in middle. Add yeast, the sugar, ¼ cup of the milk and mix. Place dough in a clean bowl that has been lightly coated with oil, cover with a clean, damp dish towel, and set aside to rise in a warm, draft-free place for 1 to 2 hours.
2. Add salt and margarine and mix well, or until dough falls easily from bowl. Cover and set aside to rise again (about 45 minutes). After it rises, roll dough into a 12 × 16-inch rectangle.
3. Mix ingredients for filling. Spread mixture on the rectangular-shaped dough. Roll dough carefully, beginning at the long side of the rectangle. Shape roll into wreath, place gently on greased pan, and mold the ends together tightly. Take a knife and mark the outer edges of the wreath slightly, about every inch. Let rise again for 20 minutes. Preheat oven to 350 degrees F.
4. Bake about 40 minutes. Set aside to cool.
5. Mix confectioners' sugar and lemon juice for glaze and spread on the cooled wreath. Decorate with colorful sugar eggs.

Serve freshly baked.

MAKES 10 TO 12 SERVINGS.

Among the Livonians many ancient Easter customs still thrive. It was believed, for example, that you would have a plentiful fishing season if firewood and chips were bought in before sunrise on Good Friday morning. Broad and thin chips meant a plentiful supply of sole, while thick logs attracted big, fat fish. Also, the Livonian fishermen would secretly smoke their nets over an anthill on the morning of Maundy Thursday to ensure a fine catch. Easter Sunday saw many Livonians at the seashore to "awaken the birds" and offer sacrifices like spirits, white bread, and sugar to Mother Sea. The following *Kliņģeris,* which is also the traditional Latvian birthday cake, is often served.

~~~⊛~~~

Traditional Latvian Birthday Cake
Kliņģeris

cups very warm milk (120 to 130 degrees F) or
    ¼ cup warm water and 2 cups warm cream
1 teaspoon saffron
5¼ cups wheat flour
½ teaspoon salt
(¼-ounce) packages dry yeast
14 tablespoons (1¾ stick) butter or margarine
egg yolks
1 cup sugar
vanilla
cardamom
dried lemon or orange peel
ginger
½ cup raisins
tablespoons cinnamon
tablespoons candied peel
almonds
confectioners' sugar

1. Mix warm milk, saffron, wheat flour, and salt together. In a separate bowl, dissolve yeast in warm water by letting it stand for 5 minutes. Add yeast to flour. Knead dough well. Cover with a damp, clean dish towel and set aside in a warm, draft-free place (about 80 degrees F) to rise for 1 to 2 hours. (If the room is cold, place pan of covered dough on rack over a large pan of hot, steaming water.)

2. Mix butter, 2 of the egg yolks, sugar, vanilla, cardamom, dried lemon peel, and ginger to taste. Beat until foamy. Add to dough. Knead.
3. Mix raisins, cinnamon, and candied peel. Knead into dough. Add flour if necessary. Set aside to rise again for 45 minutes.
4. Roll out dough about ½ inch thick. Roll into a long sausage. Twist into a pretzel shape or a figure 8 and place on cooking dish. Let rise again for 20 minutes. Brush with 1 beaten egg yolk. Sprinkle with almonds.
5. Preheat oven to 350 degrees F. Bake for 30 to 40 minutes. Before serving, sprinkle with confectioners' sugar.

MAKES 10 TO 15 SERVINGS.

Visu gradu Jānīts jāja,
Nu atjāja šovakar:
Rībēj zeme nolecot,
Šķindēj pieši atjājot.

The whole year long Jānis came riding.
Now tonight he has arrived.
The earth shakes as he dismounts.
His spurs jangle as he arrives.

—Latvian folk song

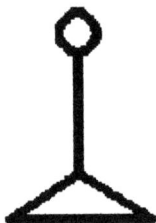

Jānis represents fertility.

Possibly the most popular pre-Christian festival still surviving in Latvia is Jāņi, which is celebrated on June 24, the longest day of the year. A time when the world of men and of gods come together, this festival of nature has been the longest ongoing tradition in Latvia and was celebrated even when it was illegal to do so. Customs still practiced today involve calling upon the spirits of the home, field, and forest to bring forth a bountiful harvest and shield the crops and livestock from witches and devils.

Everyone goes to the countryside to celebrate Jāņi with singing, dancing, and general tomfoolery. We headed to our friend Ieva's farmhouse, where her mother was already decorating the house and barn with greenery. Technically, celebrations begin the day before

Jāņi, or Līgo (Day of grass), when nature is at its most powerful. In ancient times the celebration was simply called Līgo; only after Christianity arrived did the following day become St. John's Day, or Jāņi. Herb and grasses gathered on Līgo are considered to have extra magical and spiritual powers and are dried to use for tea and dishes year-round. (In Rīga, Dome Square hosts songs, traditional dances—and plenty of grasses—on Līgo.) Placing plants around your home harnesses their power and ensures good fortune and life-giving forces throughout the year. For example, Sumac, which wards off evil spirits, is placed over the door to dispel evil thoughts from entering. When you gather it for Jāņi, you must circle the house several times to provide extra protection. Ferns evoke fertility, and oak branches worn by the men summon prosperity. Both the oak tree, the strongest tree in the forest, and the linden, which signifies the female, are regaled with song throughout the day. Stinging nettles placed under house mats ward off witches. Mountain ash twigs, thistles, and various sharp objects, usually placed over building entrances, also ward off witches and evil spirits.

The grasses aren't only for the house. Every living creature—horses, people, cows, chickens—yes, we humans too—partakes in the power of nature and spends the day and evening bedecked with garlands. The stables—even the chicken coops—are also decorated with dried garlands. Latvians save these garlands, which you can see even in the fanciest apartments in Rīga, until the next Jāņi, when they are burned to dispel any evil spirits hovering about from the past year.

Jāņi, as the longest day of the year, celebrates the day of the sun's greatest strength and the general energy of light. At about 11 P.M., after we'd decorated the house and eaten an enormous feast, the sun was only just setting. Witches and spirits are most apt to linger during this twilight hour. We lit the Jāņi bonfire for protection. You must be careful to stay in the bonfire light throughout the night because the forces of evil idle where the light from the bonfire doesn't shine. You must also stay awake. To fall asleep on Jāņi means that you'll sleep all year-round.

Perhaps the most important part of the evening is song. Songs accompany every activity from the gathering of the grasses to the lighting of the bonfire. Not only do they bless the land and people, but they include spell-making formulas to evoke fertility and protect from evil spirits as well; there are nearly 3,000 dainas for Jāņi celebrations alone. Within and in-between songs, wishes are made for fertility and prosperity. The host generally wishes for barley—to make plenty of beer—and strong horses. In keeping with tradition, we jumped over the fire to cleanse ourselves for the new year. As Jāņi is also the name day for everyone named John, anyone named John or Jānis is expected to jump several times for good luck.

Just before midnight, while it was still Līgo, we left our bonfire and walked—singing— and armed with Jāņi cheese and pīrāgi and herbs and grasses to the neighboring farms. We presented these gifts to the neighbors while singing before their bonfire, and they cheerfully sang back, offering glasses of home-brewed Jāņi beer. Cheese is eaten so that cows may thrive, and beer is drunk for the horses. After several glasses and songs, we headed to the next farm before returning home to wait for the sunrise.

Jānīts nāca pa kalniņu
Zāļu nasta mugurā.
Nāc, Jānīti, no kalniņa,
Dod manām telītēm;
Es tev došu siera nuku
Par telīšu baŗošanu.

Jāņis came over the hillside
A bundle of grass on his back.
Come dear Jāņis down the hill
Give the grass to my heifers;
I shall give you a chunk of cheese
For feeding my heifers.

—Latvian folk song

A Jāņi reveler.

Jāņi Cheese

5 quarts milk (about 20 cups)
2 pounds farmer's cheese
1 teaspoon caraway
½ cup clotted milk or yogurt (optional)
2 or 3 tablespoons butter
2 or 3 eggs, beaten with a pinch of salt

1. Bring milk to a boil. Grind cottage cheese and caraway in a food processor. If you prefer crumbly cheese, add eggs to cheese here. For a stickier cheese, add more butter and be sure that cheese is kept hot throughout the cooking process.
2. Set over low heat until cheese begins to separate. Add the clotted milk or yogurt if the cottage cheese tastes too sweet.
3. Remove from heat. Drain water. Remove cheese mass from the pan and place on cheese-cloth. Press moisture from cheese.
4. In a separate pan, melt butter. Add the cheese, beaten eggs and cook over medium heat until the mixture is yellow and thick.
5. Place mixture on cheesecloth and press out moisture.

Serve with honey and bread.

MAKES 8 TO 12 SERVINGS.

Martin's roosters

Martinš is the protector of warriors who guard the farms.

Kekatas and Martinš Day

The masked procession of Kekatas begins on November 10 with the celebration of Martinš Day and culminates around Christmas time. On Martinš Day, a day to respect the dead, candles and flowers adorn the cemeteries throughout the day and night. In the old days farmers would kill a rooster, give its blood to the horses to drink, and cook the rest for themselves on Martinš Day. The wives would do the same with a hen. Traditionally Ghosts' Visiting Time extended from September 29, or Michaelmas, to St. Martin's Day.

These days, singing, stomping (to stomp out all the weeds from the fields), and dancing revelers or *kekatnieki*, armed with homemade noisemakers, travel the neighborhoods calling on friends and neighbors. The merry *kekatnieki* wear costumes that center upon traditional folklore figures like the bear (for the mythical Lāčplēsis, a symbol of bravery), a sheaf of grain (prosperity), and the stork (fertility) and represent good spirits who will bring luck to people and fertility to the fields and livestock.

Popular dishes at Martinš are sauerkraut, Martini balls, and poultry.

Traditional Stewed or Roasted Poultry

Place a rooster or chicken (including head) in a saucepan with enough water to cover it. Bring water to boil. Add preferred (unpeeled) vegetables, such as carrots, turnips, beets, or boiled peas. Serve when poultry is cooked through.

Peas Snowball
Martini balls

When hemp was legal, it was widely used in Latvian cuisine. This recipe was made with ¼ cup hemp cooked in a frying pan over low heat until very flavorful. The roasted hemp was then ground and added to the mixture before the balls were formed. Today hemp butter is still popular.

1 cup dried peas
salt
3 or 4 potatoes, peeled and diced
a few slices smoked bacon, cut in small pieces
1 onion, chopped
3 tablespoons hemp-seed butter (optional)
1 tablespoon flour

1. Soak the peas in water overnight.
2. Boil peas in 8 cups water and salt until soft, 4 to 10 minutes. Boil potatoes with a pinch of salt until tender, 20 to 40 minutes. While peas and potatoes are still hot, grind them in a food processor.
3. Fry bacon with onions. Add hemp-seed butter if desired, flour, and a pinch of salt. Mix all ingredients.

4. Make small balls out of mixture. Place on greased baking dish and heat in 350 degrees F oven for 20 to 30 minutes before serving.

Serve with sour milk, kefir, whole milk, or buttermilk or as a side dish with meat.

MAKES 3 TO 4 SERVINGS.

Ziemassvetki

Food is prepared for many days before the four-day Ziemassvetki ("winter festival"), which is Christmas. Among the most traditional foods are pig snout, bacon rolls, barley sausage, rassols salad, and boiled peas. Traditions include the symbolic burning of the Yule log to end all the misfortunes from the past year as well as running around the house three times to prevent toothaches in the coming year. You must also step outside your house before a stranger enters on Christmas morning or he'll bring a year of unhappiness.

Rassols Salad

7 boiled potatoes, peeled and cut in small pieces
1 pound beets, peeled and cut in small pieces
1 or 2 apples, peeled and cut in small pieces
¼ cup chopped pickles (about 1 to 3 pickles)
1 to 2 salt herrings
3 eggs, hard-boiled and cut in small pieces
1 teaspoon salt
pepper

1. Mix potatoes, beets, apples, pickles, herring, eggs, and salt. Add salt and pepper to taste.

MARINADE:
2 tablespoon oil
2 tablespoon red wine vinegar
1 teaspoon salt

2. Mix oil, vinegar, salt, and 1 to 2 tablespoons water. Add to salad and mix well.
3. Refrigerate before serving.

FINAL PREPARATION:
1 cup sour cream
1 tablespoon hot mustard
salt
pepper

4. Mix sour cream and mustard. Add salt and pepper to taste. Mix with salad and serve.

MAKES 7 TO 9 SERVINGS.

Barley Sausage

¼ to ½ pound bacon
½ to ¾ pound barley grits
oil for frying
1 onion, chopped fine
sausage casing

1. Cut bacon into cubes. Wash barley grits.
2. In a frying pan, heat oil. Fry bacon and grits together until slightly brown.
3. Bring 3 cups water to boil. Add onion, bacon, and barley. Cover tightly. Boil over medium heat until onion is soft.
4. Pack filling into sausage casing.

May be served hot or cold.

MAKES 3 TO 4 SERVINGS.

The Mountaineer

Then friends depart, first one and then the other,
And solitude grows with each passing year.
Now no companion walks with you like a brother,
No hillside flower blooms to bring you cheer.

The peak is lost in mountain height,
Eternal stillness turns your heart to stone.
No place remains for rest or respite.
A shield of ice entombs your soul like ore,
While earthly longing burns in flesh and bone.

—Jānis Rainis (1865-1929), Latvian poet

BIBLIOGRAPHY

City Paper-The Baltic States. City Paper OÜ. Tallinn, Estonia. Spring and summer editions.

Latvia, The Book Latvia, Inc. 4N013 Randall Road, St. Charles, Illinois, 1984.

Latvia Agent's Manual 1ṛ. Latvian Tourist Board. 1998.

Latvia-Baltic State. Izdevniecība Baltika Ltd. 1998 #4.

Latviešu Tradicionālā Piensaimniecība. Dumpe, Linda. Latvijas vēstures instytūta apgāds, Rīga 1998.

Linguistics and Poetics of Latvian Folk Songs: Essays in Honour of the Sesquicentennial of the Birth of Kr. Barons. Edited by Vaira Vīķis-Freibergs. McGill-Queen's University Press. 1989. Kingston and Montreal, Canada.

The Story of Riga. Kolbergs, Andris. Jāņa Sēta Publishers and Printers Ltd., Riga 1998.

The Baltic Times Riga Downtown. Nr. 1- Spring 1ṛ. Baltic News Ltd. Riga, Latvia.

Translations

Translations are taken from *Linguistics and Poetics of Latvian Folk Songs: Essays in Honour of the sesquicentennial of the Birth of Kr. Barons.* Edited by Vaira Vīķis-Freibergs. McGill-Queen's University Press. 1989. Kingston and Montreal, Canada.

Breads and Pīrāgi

Māte, Māte, mīļa māte ... Muižniece, Lalita. "Linguistic Analysis of Latvian Death and Burial Songs." Doctoral dissertation, 1981. University of Michigan, Ann Arbor.

Pērkons brauca pa jūriņu ... Katzenelenbogen, Uria. *The Daina, An Anthology of Lithuanian and Latvian Folk Song*, Chicago: Lithuanian News Publishing. Excerpted from Albert B. Lord. *Theories of Oral Literature and the Latvian Dainas.*

Lād man ļaudis, buŗ man ļaudis ... Pērkons brauca pa jūriņu ... Vīķis-Freibergs, Vaira. *The Major Gods and Goddesses of Ancient Latvian Mythology.*

Soups and Porridges

Kādu Laim mūžu lika ... Vīķis-Freibergs, Vaira. *The Major Gods and Goddesses of Ancient Latvian Mythology.*

Pancakes, Egg Dishes, and Cheeses

Ābeļkoka laivu daru ... Rūķe-Draviņa, Velta. *The Apple tree in Latvian Folk Songs.*

Drinks

Ai Laimiņ licējiņa ... Lai raudāja, kas raudāja ... Katzenelenbogen, Uria. *The Daina, An Anthology of Lithuanian and Latvian Folk Song.* Chicago: Lithuanian News Publishing. Excerpted from Albert B. Lord's *Theories of Oral Literature and the Latvian Dainas.*

Salads

Augstāk dzied cīrulīts ... Vīķis-Freibergs, Vaira. *The Major Gods and Goddesses of Ancient Latvian Mythology.*

Es piesēju kumeliņu ... Rūķe-Draviņa, Velta. *The Apple Tree in Latvian Folk Songs.* Translated by Vaira Vīķis-Freibergs.

Potatoes

Mēnestiņis zvaigznes skaita ... Katzenelenbogen, Uria. *The Daina, An Anthology of Lithuanian and Latvian Folk Song*, Chicago: Lithuanian News Publishing. Excerpted from Albert B. Lord's *Theories of Oral Literature and the Latvian Dainas*.

Vēl Laimīt man mūžiņ ... Rūķe-Draviņa, Velta. *The Apple tree in Latvian Folk Songs*.

Meat Dishes

Noriet saule vakarāi ... Katzenelenbogen, Uria. *The Daina, An Anthology of Lithuanian and Latvian Folk Song*, Chicago: Lithuanian News Publishing. Excerpted from Albert B. Lord's *Theories of Oral Literature and the Latvian Dainas*.

Kālabad ik vakara ... Vīķis-Freibergs, Vaira. *Text Variants in the Latvian Folk Song Corpus: Theortetical and Practical Problems*.

Desserts

Es atradu uz celiņa ... Vīķis-Freibergs, Vaira. *The Major Gods and Goddesses of Ancient Latvian Mythology*.

Silā man rudzi sēti ... Eckert, Rainer. *Ancient Bee-Keeping Terminology in Kr. Barons' Collection Latvju Dainas*. Translated by Vaira Vīķis-Freibergs.

Visapkārt ievu ziedi ... Rūķe-Draviņa, Velta. *The Apple Tree in Latvian Folk Songs*.

Holiday Foods

Visu gradu Jānīts jāja ... Jānīts nāca pa kalniņu ... Vīķis-Freibergs, Vaira. *The Major Gods and Goddesses of Ancient Latvian Mythology*.

INDEX

Baltic Language Dictionaries & Learning Guides from Hippocrene Books . . .

Latvian-English/English Latvian Practical Dictionary
M. Sosare and I. Birzvalka
This completely modern dictionary contains 16,000 entries and includes phrases and idiomatic expressions. Phonetic transcription is given in the English-Latvian section. Clear and comprehensive, this dictionary will prove an invaluable communication tool for both Latvians living in North America and for native English speaking students, travelers and businesspeople.
16,000 entries • 286 pages • 4½ x 7 • 0-7818-0059-5 • $16.95pb • (194)

Lithuanian-English/English-Lithuanian Concise Dictionary
Victoria Martsinkyavitshute
• Over 8,000 entries
• Comprehensive definitions
• Phonetics for both languages
• Concise, easy-to-use format
• Completely modern
• Parts of speech indicated
8,000 entries • 382 pages • 4 x 6 • 0-7818-0151-6 • $14.95pb • (489)
Also available in *Compact* size: 3 x 4½ • 0-7818-0536-8 • $8.95pb • (624)

Beginner's Lithuanian
L. Dambriunas, A. Klimas, W.R. Schmalstieg
A perfect introduction to the Lithuanian language, this book is a comprehensive learning guide and teaching tool. Includes 40 lessons, a complete grammar section, review lessons, and comprehensive vocabulary lists.
471 pages • 6 x 9 • 0-7818-0678-X • $19.95pb • (764)

Estonian-English/English-Estonian Concise Dictionary
Ksana Kyiv & Oleg Benyuch
• Over 10,000 entries
• Comprehensive definitions
• Phonetics for both languages
• Detailed index of geographical names
• Transliteration guides
• Notes on Estonian cuisine
10,000 entries • 180 pages • 4 x 6 • 0-87052-081-4 • $11.95pb • (379)

Cookbooks of interest from Hippocrene . . .

The Art of Lithuanian Cooking
Maria Gieysztor de Gorgey
This volume of over 150 authentic Lithuanian recipes includes such classic favorites as Fresh Cucumber Soup, Lithuanian Meat Pockets, Hunter's Stew, Potato Zeppelins, as well as delicacies like Homemade Honey Liqueur and Easter Gypsy Cake. The author's introduction and easy step-by-step instructions ensure that even novice cooks can create authentic, delicious Lithuanian recipes.
230 pages • 5½ x 8¼ • 0-7818-0610-7 • $24.95hc • (722)

The Best of Scandinavian Cooking: Danish, Norwegian and Swedish
Shirley Sarvis & Barbara Scott O'Neil
This exciting collection of 100 recipes, each dish the favorite of a Scandinavian cook, spans the range of home cooking—appetizers, soups, omelets, pancakes, meats and pastries. Included are directions for making such tempting dishes as Norwegian Blueberry Omelet, Danish Butter Cake, Swedish Pancakes with Ligonberries—and a section entitled "A Smørrebrød Sampling," devoted to those openfaced Danish sandwiches. Each recipe has been carefully tested with North American ingredients and measures.
142 pages • 5½ x 8¼ • 0-7818-0547-3 • $9.95pb • (643)

Good Food from Sweden
Inga Norberg
This classic of Swedish cookery includes recipes for fish and meat dishes, vegetables, breads and sweets, including cookies, cakes, candies and syrups. A large section is dedicated to the savory tidbits included in the traditional Swedish smorgasbord.
192 pages • 5½ x 8¼ • 0-7818-0486-8 • $10.95pb • (544)

The Best of Smorgasbord Cooking
Gerda Simonson
Recipes for the traditional Swedish smorgasbord, including meat and game dishes, aspics and salads, fish, pastas and vegetables.
158 pages • 5½ x 8¼ • 0-7818-0407-8 • $14.95pb • (207)

All prices subject to change without prior notice. **To purchase Hippocrene Books** contact your local bookstore, call (718) 454-2366, or write to: HIPPOCRENE BOOKS, 171 Madison Avenue, New York, NY 10016. Please enclose check or money order, adding $5.00 shipping (UPS) for the first book and $.50 for each additional book.